8 KEYS TO SAFE TRAUMA RECOVERY

ALSO BY BABETTE ROTHSCHILD FROM W.W. NORTON

The Body Remembers (2000)

The Body Remembers Casebook (2003)

Help for the Helper (2006)

8 KEYS TO SAFE TRAUMA RECOVERY

Take-Charge Strategies to Empower Your Healing

_____

BABETTE ROTHSCHILD

W. W. Norton

New York ·London

Contact the author at:
Babette Rothschild
PO Box 241783
Los Angeles, CA 90024
310.281.9646
babette@8keys.cc
Visit Babette's Web site at http://www.trauma.cc and the online Safe Trauma
Recovery community at www.safetraumarecovery.com.

For information about permission to reproduce selections from this book, write to
Permissions, W. W. Norton & Company, Inc., 500 Fifth Avenue, New York, NY 10110

For information about special discounts for bulk purchases, please contact W. W.
Norton Special Sales at specialsales@wwnorton.com or 800-233-4830

Manufacturing by World Color, Fairfield Graphics
Book design by Jonathan Lippincott
Production manager: Leeann Graham

Library of Congress Cataloging-in-Publication Data

Rothschild, Babette.
8 keys to safe trauma recovery : take-charge strategies to empower your healing /
Babette Rothschild. — 1st ed.
p.   cm.
Includes bibliographical references and index.
ISBN 978-0-393-70605-5 (pbk.)
1. Psychic trauma—Treatment.   I. Title.   II. Title: Eight keys to safe trauma
recovery.
RC552.T7R68   2010
616.85'21—dc22   2009028476

ISBN: 978-0-393-70605-5 (pbk.)
W. W. Norton & Company, Inc., 500 Fifth Avenue, New York, N.Y. 10110
www.wwnorton.com
W. W. Norton & Company, Ltd., Castle House, 75/76 Wells Street, London W1T 3QT

4   5   6   7   8   9   0

This book is dedicated to the memory of
Lone Reimert
and
Lennart Ollars
Beloved therapists and teachers from my 9 years of study,
work, growth, and adventure in Denmark. Thank you for your
enduring support and for enabling me to recover from—and
learn so much about—trauma from the inside out.

Contents

Preface: Common Sense and Trauma Recovery ix

Acknowledgments xiii

Introduction 1

KEY 1: Plot Your Course With Mindfulness 7

KEY 2: Begin With Your Epilogue . . . You Made It! 27

KEY 3: Remembering Is *Not* Required 41

KEY 4: Stop Flashbacks 59

KEY 5: Reconcile Forgiveness and Shame 73

      Part A. Forgive Your Limitations 73

      Part B. Share Your Shame 87

KEY 6: Take Smaller Steps for Bigger Leaps 101

KEY 7: Get Moving 115

KEY 8: Make Lemonade 131

Afterword: Evaluating Recovery Progress 145

Further Reading 149

Notes to Self-Help Readers 151

Notes to Past, Present, and Future Clients of Trauma Therapy 153

Notes to Trauma Treatment Professionals 157

Index 161

Preface: Common Sense and Trauma Recovery

Common sense is the foundation of everything I write and teach, and has become a popular topic at my trainings. Merriam-Webster's 11th *Collegiate Dictionary* defines common sense as "sound and prudent judgment based on a simple perception of the situation or facts." As straightforward as it sounds, common sense can be very difficult to nail down and apply. In fact, one of my closest friends, Michael Gavin (in London), often reminds me that "common sense is *not* very common." Unfortunately, I have to agree with him, particularly when dealing with trauma.

Questions have burned in me during and since my own recovery from PTSD and throughout my professional studies: Why did the route to my healing have to be so brutal at times? Having suffered during the trauma, was it really necessary to suffer again while attempting to heal from it? Why did it seem that dealing with the effects of trauma involved nearly the same level of terror and distress as the original events? My own common sense screamed that there must be additional options for trauma recovery, ways to make it safer and less traumatic.

Primarily, it is my aim to reduce the trauma of self-help recovery and trauma therapy. It is of concern to me that so many people find, as I did, healing from trauma to be as horrendous as—or sometimes even more horrendous than—the actual incidents.[1] Most traumatic events last a relatively short span of time, but their wounds can fester for a lifetime when recovery options are unavailable, limited, or misapplied.

After many years of working with traumatized clients, supervising trauma professionals, reading the available trauma literature and research extensively, and dealing with my own past, I have concluded that the bottom line of trauma recovery involves only a few key issues:

- Recognition that the trauma survivor actually did survive the trauma
- Understanding that a flashback is a memory
- Self-forgiveness for not being able to prevent or stop what occurred
- Alleviation of shame
- Reducing recovery steps to manageable size
- Mobilizing the body out of a frozen or defeated state
- Extracting meaning or purpose from the trauma to better oneself and/or one's world

You may notice that *remembering the trauma* is not a part of this list. I question the regular practice of investigating and revisiting trauma memories over and over again. Most people assume this is necessary for everyone, but that goes against common sense. For some it is quite helpful, but for others it is disastrous. Moreover, processing the details of what occurred is not always (or even usually) necessary to resolve the other issues. In fact, people who recover from trauma on their own tend to have much less intense memory of their traumas and are free of the need to repeatedly remember or track down every detail. It is also significant to note that a good portion of trauma victims suffer a worsening of symptoms when encouraged or forced to remember their traumas.

---

[1]Throughout this text, either the singular or plural forms of *trauma*, *incident*, and *event* are used depending on the context. Please edit in your own mind as you read—whether you have experienced one or multiple traumas—to fit your individual situation.

There is a critical misperception that to recover from trauma, you must feel worse before you can get better. This is another belief that goes against common sense. If remembering makes someone worse, then they are likely to do best by avoiding their memories, at least as long as those memories hurt rather than heal. The goal of trauma healing must be to *relieve*, not intensify, suffering. Common sense requires improving quality of life to be the primary goal. Revisiting the horrors of the past should only be a part of the process when it serves this goal. That is not to say that trauma survivors should always feel good. That would not make any sense either. In recovering from any painful condition, there will be periods of discomfort. However, the discomfort of recovering from trauma must never compromise the individual's life quality or ability to function normally on a day-to-day basis.

A central principle of common sense I have always abided by is not to expect any two individuals to be alike. This includes traumatized individuals and their responses to recovery interventions. I would never expect one strategy to work exactly the same with two people. Recovery proceeds best when common sense is liberally applied to tailor any approach or program to the unique needs of each individual trauma survivor.

I have endeavored to fill this book with common sense and demystify the process of trauma recovery. I hope it significantly contributes to your supply of tools and confidence to manage and achieve your healing.

Acknowledgments

A few weeks before completing this manuscript, I had an enlightening cyber interchange with my Irish friend, Patricia Bourke, also named below for her helpful literary feedback. That day our text messaging had nothing to do with this book, but some point or other about which I was being persistent. She sent back a text calling me "encouragable" instead of "incorrigible." At first I laughed, but then I became intrigued. She had invented a new word and I liked it. Fairly quickly, I decided it should mean "someone who encourages" and the first person who came to mind was my editor, Deborah Malmud, the most "encouragable" person I know. Actually, the definition easily applies to everyone I have worked with at W. W. Norton over the last decade, including Kevin Olsen, Elisabeth Kerr, Kristen Holt-Browning, Vani Kannan, Andrea Costella, Bev Benzeleski, Kathryn Pinto, and also Susan Munro and Michael McGandy, who have both moved on to other pursuits. I could not ask for a better editor or publisher or more support for my writing projects. I count them among my blessings daily.

Really, everyone who has helped me shape this book has been incredibly "encouragable." I owe many, many thanks to those who took the time to read and critique the first and second drafts: Jeanne Ladner, David Grill, Robin Petro, Sima Stanley, Victoria Haviland, Patricia Bourke, Gillford d'Souza, and Karin Rhines. This book is very much the better for their candid feedback.

Introduction

My professional goal has always been to become obsolete, that is, no longer needed. I would be most happy to achieve this goal as a result of the elimination of trauma from the world. But since that is not likely, I will settle for becoming unneeded because traumatized individuals are extremely well prepared — informed and equipped — to direct their own healing. I hope that *8 Keys to Safe Trauma Recovery* will make a significant contribution toward achieving that goal. It is my aim for this book to supply you with essential knowledge and tools that will make your recovery from trauma a safe journey.

Why do I keep using the term *safe* when I talk about trauma recovery? As most of you reading this book already know, recovering from trauma is fraught with difficulty. Missteps are easy to come by. Most self-help books offer only a single approach.

Likewise, trauma treatment programs and trauma therapists tend to favor just one method. So when you invest time and money in self-help books or therapy sessions, it is easy to feel obliged to stick with whatever you have chosen. When you are lucky, it will be something that suits you. However, when you are not, you could feel responsible for the failure: "What's wrong with me that this didn't work?" Frustration is the best outcome in such situations; a degraded degree of functioning is the worst.

However, there is another way to approach this dilemma, to make trauma recovery safer. I want to help put you in the driver's seat, so to speak, of your own trauma recovery and to equip you with the controls you need to reach your goal safely, whether you are just beginning your healing or have been working at it for a while. When you take control, you might decide to use a little from this and a lot from that—whatever combination it is that you find works *for you*. Trauma makes you feel out of control. Taking charge of your own course of recovery will help you to reclaim control over yourself, your symptoms, and your life. These eight keys are a contribution toward that end.

Trauma recovery involves much more than remembering and processing the traumatizing incidents. In fact, for some of you, focusing on the past will not be necessary, or desirable. Trauma recovery must, first and foremost, *improve your quality of life*. Anything which furthers that goal is good for you; anything which compromises that goal is not. That may sound very simplistic, but in a way this principle is just that simple. Toward that goal, each of the eight keys is designed to:

- Increase your information about trauma
- Add to your self-knowledge
- Contribute to the calming of your nervous system so you can think more clearly and make decisions more easily

These keys will make it possible for you to access your own common sense and the wisdom of your body and mind. Thus armed, you will be able to make informed judgments about what is and what is not good for you, what furthers your recovery and improves your quality of life versus what compromises them. You can use any or all of the eight keys alone or in conjunction with whichever additional self-help or professional recovery books or programs you pursue.

What Is Successful Recovery?

At this point you may be wondering what successful recovery from trauma looks like. I will sketch criteria here and expand on the points throughout the book and in the Afterword beginning on page 145. There are at least two ways to measure your success, both necessary aspects of your evaluation:

- *Objective measures of success* include behaviors that anyone can see, for instance, going back to work, eating normally, expanding activities that were restricted, and so on. The particulars of what you will be measuring depends on how trauma has affected your daily life.
- *Subjective measures of success* are 100% determined by you. Do you feel adequately improved? Is your day-to-day functioning as you want it? Are you in control of your previous symptoms? For example, have you gained mastery over flashbacks and the ability to calm yourself, and are you more at peace within your own mind and body?

Book Structure

Eight Keys to Safe Trauma Recovery is organized with an eye to accessibility and ease of use. Each chapter covers one key and includes nine central elements:

1. A description of the issue the chapter's key will address.
2. A composite case example to introduce the problems the key is intended to unlock.
3. Discussion of the problems, introducing theory as appropriate.
4. Description of the key.
5. One or more examples of applying the key to the composite case.

6. Guidance in the form of advice, questions, or a check-list to help you decide if you should go forward with one or more of the exercises.
7. Three or more exercises for practice in using the key.
8. Questions together with guided mindfulness to enable evaluation of the key's personal benefit. Placement of this section in each chapter will help to reinforce one of the core principles of 8 *Keys to Safe Trauma Recovery*: Always evaluate philosophies and techniques carefully, including those in *this* book.
9. The last section will guide readers in implementation and continued evaluation of the key in their daily life.

Reader Assurance

To the best of my ability, I have eliminated material that has an obvious potential to distress readers. Discussion of types of trauma and examples of traumatized individuals are limited to brief, outline-type descriptions, eliminating the kinds of detail that many would find upsetting. It is my wish to demonstrate in these pages that trauma recovery does not need to be traumatic. That said, of course I cannot predict particular areas of sensitivity or triggers of individual readers. However, please know that if something herein provokes or upsets you, it was *not* intended for that purpose. You can read with confidence that each word and situation is carefully chosen and edited to optimize the highest level of information and interest, while minimizing potential reader discomfort.

Correspondence and Feedback

My contact information is included on the copyright page at the front of this book. I welcome your feedback, both positive and negative. At the same time, I may not be able to answer every e-mail or letter, although I will do my best to acknowledge your communication. Remember also that neither e-mail nor the postal service are perfect systems. Sometimes letters and messages go astray. So if you do not receive a reply from me, please do not take it as a rejection. Assume that either I did not receive your note, or for other reasons I was unable to respond. Also, please do not send long letters that include intimate details of personal history—someone else might be able to read what you wrote (the Internet is much more public than most people realize). If you would like a response, the more concise your communication, the better.

Disclaimer

It is now a tradition for me to add a disclaimer to all of my books as well as at the start of all my lectures and trainings.

The information discussed and interventions suggested in this book are all based on theory, hypothesis, and speculation. This is because everything in the trauma field *is* theory and speculation. There is nothing we know for sure, no hard facts. Actually, this is also the case for all of psychology and even much (if not most) of science and medicine. Beliefs change all the time as new information is discovered and digested. My own physician once reminded me that in medicine, "today's gospel is tomorrow's heresy." We see evidence of that frequently, as treatments and medications are introduced and withdrawn. The same applies in trauma recovery. More importantly, it is not wise to assume that what works for one individual will work for another. The best trauma recovery program for you will be the one that is tailored to your individual needs.

In Denmark they say that when you get a new piece of information you should "chew on it," *at tygge på*. If it does not taste good, you should spit it out immediately. However, if it tastes okay, then just swallow a little and see how it digests before swallowing the whole thing. I would never expect—or even want—a reader to swallow everything I write. I do not even believe that to be healthy. I hope that you will taste what is offered in these pages and absorb and use only that which digests comfortably and makes sense for you.

One of my favorite slogans is, "I get paid for my opinion, not to be right." At the end of the day, or in this case, this book, all I—or, for that matter, any author or therapist—have to offer you are my opinions. Of course, considered, informed, professional opinions are important in evaluating your situation and planning and carrying out your recovery. But do not mistake opinions for facts. Just because an expert quotes research or other scientific evidence that strategy or intervention X, Y, and Z are the best, there is no guarantee that all (or even any) of them will suit or be right for *you*. You are ultimately the best expert about yourself. Adopt only those opinions that fit with what you know about yourself. That is the way for you to best ensure your safe recovery from trauma.

PLOT YOUR COURSE
WITH MINDFULNESS

The range of what we think and do is limited by what we fail to notice. And because we fail to notice that we fail to notice there is little we can do to change until we notice how failing to notice shapes our thoughts and deeds.

—R. D. LAING

The ultimate value of life depends upon awareness, and the power of contemplation rather than upon mere survival.   —ARISTOTLE

While currently escalating in popularity, the practice of mindfulness is not new. With roots in Buddhism and Eastern philosophy, mindfulness was first introduced to psychology in the 1900s through Gestalt therapy and the somatic psychologies. Since the 1990s, mindfulness has increasingly gained respect as a tried and true asset for trauma recovery. It is even now advocated by many in the mainstream of trauma treatment and research. The purpose of this chapter is to highlight particular principles of mindfulness that are useful for healing and for plotting your course of recovery. For that reason, the discussion of mindfulness per se is limited here. It will not include mindfulness as a meditation or spiritual practice.

The concept of mindfulness is, at least on the surface, quite simple. It is basically a focused self-knowledge that includes several facets—awareness of body sensations (temperature, tension, butterflies in the stomach), states (hungry, sleepy), feelings (happy, sad), images, and thoughts—as they move in and out of your consciousness. As such, mindfulness enables you to access all sorts of data about yourself. To aid trauma recovery, any single facet or combination of them will be particularly useful.

Probably you have already used mindfulness in your daily life, perhaps even on a regular basis. Attending to your feelings or your body's reactions to decide what to have for lunch or choose what you wear to work are likely examples. Usually we are not aware of how much information goes into our decision making. Buying furniture is another area where people commonly use mindfulness. Remember the last time you bought a chair or couch for a room in your home or office. On what did you base your choice? Did you sit in several to compare how they felt—hard or soft, comfortable or uncomfortable? How about how you felt in the various possibilities? Did you notice if sitting in one or the other made you feel happy, at ease, alert, or restless? Maybe you also tried to imagine how each would affect the mood of the room it was meant for, or if it would change how you felt in that room (for better or for worse). One or more of the chairs may have elicited memories of another place or time, perhaps when you saw or sat in something similar.

Choosing furniture is only one (if very basic) example of how you can apply mindfulness in a practical way. Via this chapter, it is my aim to help you to use this simple strategy to make all sorts of—and more critical—choices based on what your own "inner Goldilocks" tells you. Not only will mindfulness help you to choose the right chair, it can also guide you in the choices you make to further your trauma recovery.

Barry[1] came to me for consultation suffering from extreme

---

1. To protect privacy and confidentiality, identifying information has been altered for all case examples throughout the book (except when using my own situation for illustration). For the same reason, each example is actually a composite of several cases. In every instance I have endeavored to maintain the integrity of the actual issues and strategies being illustrated.

posttraumatic stress disorder (PTSD). You might recognize some of his symptoms: periods of rapid heartbeat, cold sweating, difficulty sleeping, difficulty concentrating, intrusive thoughts of the incident that traumatized him, and so on. One of the things I routinely suggest to those in a similar state is to pay attention to what they eat and drink. Usually, when someone is so distressed, I will recommend reducing consumption of caffeine (in coffee, tea, aspirin, and many soft drinks) and MSG (a flavor enhancer common in Asian cuisines and canned soups), both of which can increase the pulse, triggering a worsening of symptoms. But an interesting thing happened when Barry actually paid attention to the effects of what he ate. He found out that drinking a Red Bull (a highly caffeinated soft drink) calmed him more than anything else. Moreover, Chinese food was his favorite and never caused him distress. However, he found that eating an apple (which he usually did daily) and a few other common foods made him quite anxious. The results of his investigation reminded me just how different the effects of food can be on different individuals. With a little practice, Barry was able to look at something in his cupboard or on a restaurant menu and accurately predict if it would raise or lower his heart rate and other symptoms. He got very good at it. Applying mindfulness to what he ate did not cure Barry by any means, but it did help him to better control his anxiety and arousal levels, which eased his recovery process considerably. It was an important step, a helpful piece to his puzzle.

Consider the advantage of applying the same principles to even more significant choices—the value of being able to predict and evaluate which treatment, exercise, or intervention is right for you. Mindfulness can assist you in taking the power of determining what is best for you away from the "experts" and holding it firmly in your own hands (and mind and body) where it belongs. Of course, advice from specialists—authors, doctors, and therapists—will still be valuable, but with *you* able to evaluate what helps you, their counsel will be even more beneficial. There is danger in assuming that an author or therapist knows what is best for you. Mindfulness can help you to gauge if you do or do not agree with another's assessment or suggested direction. If you do not agree, you can then decide if you would rather follow your own direction or seek one or more additional opinions.

The Issue

In general, people suffering from the aftermath of trauma are very vulnerable. Their nervous systems are off-kilter. Somatic (body) and psychological (mind) symptoms are confusing and frightening. Most of these individuals become desperate to try whatever is offered to them. When something works, all the better. But when interventions fail, the trauma survivor can end up in worse condition than before treatment. The following e-mail is an example of such a treatment failure.

> Dear Babette Rothschild,
>   I've been an inpatient in a trauma recovery program for the past 7 months, diagnosed with complex PTSD. I can't say that I am much better, and everyone is frustrated because I still can't remember anything from before I was 11 years old. That is where my therapist says the trauma is, but try as I might, I can't remember. I am more and more scared that I will not get what I need here or anywhere. I hope you can advise me.
>
> > Best wishes,
> > Martha

There is something highly amiss in situations such as Martha's. She finds herself in a real jam: she has committed herself to a treatment program, but has found that *in 7 months* it is not working for her. She is still attempting to adapt to the program, but try as she might, she cannot fulfill their requirements.

I often receive e-mails similar to this one. Each writer is, like

Martha, looking for advice on how to pursue their recovery or asking my opinion on the usefulness of a particular program, method, or book. There are so many options available that it is often difficult to choose, to predict what will work. It does not help the matter that evidence for what has been "proven" to work is at times confusing and even contradictory.

Is it possible Martha could have been counseled or helped to foresee if this program would suit her or to recognize the program's ill fit before investing so much in it? There is no way to know, but mindfulness might have been useful for Martha. It is possible that had she been guided to focus attention on her body sensations, emotional reactions, and thoughts while considering inpatient programs, she would have accessed information indicating a clearer direction for her. For example, if she could have felt her stomach clutch and her feet go cold as she read (or heard) that this program required accessing trauma memories, she may have had a tangible indicator that the program might not be for her. Perhaps she would have seen a symbol in her mind's eye. Maybe a "Stop" or "Dead End" sign would have appeared to her had she known how to focus. There is no way to know, but Martha's situation illuminates one area where mindfulness has the potential to be useful in facilitating trauma recovery and plotting a course of treatment. Below is another.

The Case: Janice, Part 1

Janice wanted to be touched and held. But at the same time, she found that she would space out whenever she was in physical contact with another person. She could not stay present when holding or hugging anyone, let alone when having sexual contact. It was such a dilemma for her that she avoided becoming involved in a meaningful relationship. Instead she would sometimes take home a stranger she met at a party so that she could, as she said, "relieve my tension without anyone caring if I was there for it or not." She especially related to the scene in *Annie*

Hall where Annie's spirit leaves the bed during sex with Woody Allen's character.

Molested by her father on a regular basis since she was quite young, Janice had developed an ambivalence about touch—needing the contact, fearing the contact. As an adult, the same conflict plagued her. She felt a deep need to be touched and held, but every attempt to fulfill her need ended in either frustration or panic. When she tried to forgo touch altogether, a deep depression would set in. She needed to find some compromise. Could mindfulness be helpful?

Apply a Little Theory

The practice of mindfulness, though popularized in recent years, had its beginnings more than 2,500 years ago in the Buddhist practice of meditation. In modern times the skill has further been applied to everything from treating depression to sharpening business acumen. During the 20th century, Gestalt therapy, body psychotherapies, particularly Hakomi, and somatic treatment methods such as the Feldenkrais and the Alexander technique introduced the practice of mindfulness (including body awareness) into psychotherapy. During the early part of the 21st century, cognitive therapies have adopted mindfulness as a core of their approaches.

There are four foundations upon which Buddha taught mindfulness:

1. Body—both physical and energetic, but here we will stick to the concrete, material body, particularly somatic sensations
2. Feelings—the emotions
3. Mind—including thoughts and images
4. Dharmas—having to do with the interrelationship of all things in the world

For the purposes of this book, this key will involve specific use of the first three foundations. Students, practitioners, and masters of Buddhism and Buddhist mindfulness will likely find this discussion and application highly limited. However, this is not a book, nor even a chapter, about Buddhism. The concept of mindfulness is being applied here for a very concrete, targeted purpose. For those who want exposure to the deeper esoteric philosophy and practice, I hope that you will delve further on your own.

Basically, mindfulness involves the focus of consciousness on whatever is happening *now*, in the present time, in and around you. Thoughts, feelings, sensations, and impulses may all be targets of mindful awareness. Mindfulness can also involve the spiritual realm, but does not need to. For our purposes here, the focus will be on the body, feeling, and mind aspects of mindfulness.

To further grasp the relevance of mindfulness to trauma recovery, it may be helpful to understand Antonio Damasio's theory of *somatic markers*. Best known for his book *Descartes' Error*, Damasio developed his somatic marker theory while investigating people with a particular type of brain injury. He found some surprising commonalities among those patients who had damage in the prefrontal cortex. They had little to no awareness of body sensations, particularly their internal sensations, such as butterflies in the stomach, changes in heart rate or breathing, or heat or coolness in the skin that would indicate flushing or becoming pale. Moreover, they were unable to identify their feelings (e.g., anger, sadness, fear, happiness). And, most significantly, they could no longer make rational decisions. In linking those characteristics together, Damasio concluded that body awareness and emotional awareness are necessary to decision making. He identified that the experiences we encounter in our lives leave pleasant and unpleasant traces inscribed in our bodies—somatic markers—that help guide our future decision making. For an easy test of

Damasio's theory, go to your kitchen and, one at a time, sniff one or more of your spices or herbs—start with the one you like best. As you take in the fragrance, observe what happens in your body—is the sensation in your stomach pleasant or unpleasant? Does anything change in your breathing? Then notice if any thoughts or images from your past are associated with that spice or herb, such as Grandma's kitchen or a date at a particular restaurant. Whatever the result, the physical sensations and/or memories are all triggered by the somatic markers associated with that particular aroma. A pleasant experience will leave somatic markers that feel nice; unpleasant ones, something that is more disagreeable.

Somatic markers can be triggered by any of our senses. You might notice that sometimes the expression on your face and sensation in your gut change instantly when you first hear certain voices at the other end of the telephone line. Before you have even thought the person's name, you have memories of your last encounter. That is a response of your somatic markers to that particular voice—or, if you do not know the person, to similar voices you have had experience with in your past. I often play musical clips at lectures to demonstrate how somatic markers work. Most people have strong ones associated with music. The Beatles' "Come Together" always provides amusement for audiences who mostly were in college in the 1960s and 1970s. Hearing that song, many admit (sometimes reluctantly) to somatic markers that remind them of the smell of marijuana and to feeling a bit stoned. Somatic markers are powerful, indeed.

So what is the purpose of somatic markers and how are they relevant to mindfulness? Damasio believes that the traces left by the somatic markers from past experiences help to guide future decision making, usually acting behind our awareness. Developing and using a *mindful gauge*—a type of mindfulness for evaluating responses—will, in part, make your somatic markers conscious so you can use them for help in making decisions.

Returning to Barry's situation from the beginning of this chapter, note that he became good at seeing or imagining a food and deciding if it would be good for him to eat. This is consistent with how Damasio sees decision making. You do not have to eat or do something to predict its effect. Elements of a current decision will have somatic markers for anything similar in the past. Usually this process is going on unconsciously. However, using mindfulness, you can become aware of the factors (past and present) affecting you—identifying somatic reactions, memory images, emotions, and so on—when facing new decisions. In this way, mindfulness can be applied to decisions about your trauma recovery: direction, strategies, timing, and so forth. Using mindfulness, your somatic markers have the potential to help guide your choices.

Discovering the Key:
Janice, Part 1, Continued

Janice's touch dilemma was not a easy one. The solution was not simply one way or the other. The answer would lie in finding a balance between two extremes. I suspected that mindfulness could be a powerful tool for Janice to help her find her way through to a compromise. If I could help Janice to identify her feelings about touch and her body reactions to it, she might then be able to distinguish which she could manage and stay present for and which would send her awareness packing. With mindful observation, she would get to know how her responses changed with various types of touch, different people, and shifts of her own or the other's mind or mood. Going the mindfulness route would not be a quick fix, but would require some careful investigation on her part.

As discussed above, mindfulness involves attentiveness to the body and bodily sensations as well as feelings, thoughts, and impulses. It is through such awareness that Janice learned to identify her own mindful gauge. She then used her gauge to begin to negotiate her dilemma about touch. The initial process involved several steps.

The first mindful focus was to identify which signals were most obvious to Janice when she focused on decisions or options. I asked her to spend a week paying attention to simple tasks in her daily life such as deciding what to wear or eat. These basic choices could serve as a training ground for developing skill in this area of mindfulness. We first practiced together by having her choose a comfortable place to sit in the room with me. I asked her to move her chair to different distances and positions in relationship to the room and to where I was sitting, and to see what changed in her bodily sensations, her thoughts, or her mood. After trying several variations, she identified specific changes in her stomach sensations and also in her heart rate. When she sat close facing me directly, her heart would beat faster and her stomach felt twisted. She also noticed a picture in her mind of a scared rabbit. Moving her chair back a foot or so and turning it slightly to the right slowed her pulse. Her stomach felt more quiet and the rabbit in her mind's eye looked happy.

With several gauges identified, I suggested Janice continue practice as homework in situations where there was little to no risky emotional component. For the next week she would use heart rate, stomach sensations, and the rabbit image to help her decide which television program to watch, which toothpaste to use, what to order or bring for lunch, and so on. She thought these tasks were a bit simplistic as she was anxious to get to her touch issue. However, she agreed that the better she became at identifying fluctuations in her gauge when there was little risk of upset, the more skilled she would be in a stressful situation. I likened this training to learning to swim in the shallow end, spending some time only kicking or blowing bubbles before moving on to the deep end of the pool. The analogy made sense to her and she was able to be patient as she spent a week or so gaining proficiency in using her gauges.

The next time I saw Janice, she was much more confident.

She felt ready to use her mindful gauges to tackle her touch dilemma. The first task would be to distinguish types of touch she could manage from those which she did not or could not tolerate. To facilitate the process, Janice brought a trusted friend with her to the session. We began with Janice using mindfulness to become aware of her current state, emphasizing the gauges she had practiced using at home. This served to identify a baseline so we would know if and when anything changed. Understandably, she was slightly anxious about this new challenge. She noticed a slight increase in her heart rate and her rabbit looked guarded, though interested.

Janice then asked her friend for a hug. The friend complied and Janice immediately spaced out. It quickly became obvious that we had a third gauge: dissociation. Janice did not even hear my questions. I asked the friend to move back to her starting place and Janice slowly revived and came back into contact. This was a dramatic demonstration of her touch ambivalence. Discussing what had happened, Janice described it as becoming very dazed. She could see me and the room, but she could not hear me properly. In reviewing how she had decided to ask for a hug, Janice realized she had completely bypassed checking in with her now well-trained gauges. She had jumped to what she thought she wanted; she had not monitored her reactions to that thought. Janice was surprised when I called this first experiment a complete success. Though she thoroughly dissociated, she also learned a very useful, if uncomfortable, lesson.

It did not take long for Janice to realize herself that for the next step she needed to check with her gauges before asking. So she sat by herself a few feet from her friend and imagined getting a hug. She did not dissociate, but she could feel her heart rate go up and the bottom drop out of her stomach. The image of the rabbit in her mind froze, looking stunned. These responses told her that a hug was—at least at that moment in time—too risky. The reason could be the pressure of the situation, having me there as an observer, or that her system was just not ready for a hug in general. But none of that really mattered. Her gauges were clearly telling her, "No, not now!"

Janice became very sad. She wanted a hug but did not want to dissociate again. She felt hopeless. I had to remind her that we were just beginning and that there were many types of touch besides hugs. I encouraged Janice to imagine other kinds and degrees of touch: handshake, hand on shoulder or back, sitting side by side or back to back, touching feet, and so forth. For each imagined touch she was to, again, pay attention to her gauges. After a few minutes of imagination and gauge monitoring, Janice smiled shyly and asked her friend to just place a hand on her left shoulder. When the friend complied, Janice sighed and her eyes reddened; she did not dissociate. The contact was easy on her gauges (her heart rate stayed steady, as did her stomach; the rabbit image looked calm), though she felt sad as she knew a part of her wanted more. She was, however, pleased that she could tolerate the touch to her shoulder. And she was surprised at how much it meant to her to feel her friend's touch without it making her anxious or dazed.

On that day, Janice felt successful on two counts. She was able to trust her gauges and to use them to find a way to be touched without dissociating. All in all, she felt proud of herself. We agreed that this was not at all the last step but the first of many. (For more about Janice, see Key 3.)

Applications for You

First of all, are you ready to apply this key?

- Does this concept make sense to you?
- So far, has this chapter been calming or comfortable for you to read?

If your answer to these questions is basically positive, then you are probably ready to try this out. However, if the idea makes no sense or you have felt distressed reading this chapter, it might be best to postpone or skip the exercises that follow. Alternatively, you could read through one exercise at a time and ask the same questions above before deciding if you will attempt it. Although there will be suggestions for applying mindful gauges in later chapters, they are not required for making use of the rest of the book. It is important that you take your time and—as with the Danish concept of chewing on a new idea that I mentioned in the introduction—sample and taste before (please excuse the mixed metaphor) diving in.

For those who are ready, now it is your turn to find one or more gauges that you can use to guide you in decisions about your trauma recovery—including determining which of the keys and exercises in this book are useful to you. The next few pages include exercises to build your skill in identifying and using mindful gauges. In addition, at the end of every chapter you will have a chance to practice using your gauges to evaluate if that chapter's key is or is not useful and beneficial for you. At times you may want to use your gauge after you attempt an exercise or key. Also try using your gauge while just imagining the task, as Janice did while imagining types of touch and as Barry did when deciding what to eat. That will give you practice in predicting what might or might not help you without having to do it first. I wish Martha had been taught to do this before investing so much in a treatment program that was not suited to her needs.

Your mindful gauge will be unique. That means no one can tell you what your gauge is. Mindfulness will be your single best tool for discovering your unique gauge.

Janice discovered three gauges, but there are many, many more. I suggest additional ones below. Use my examples as inspiration to find your own unique gauge. Do not be surprised if you discover one or more that are not mentioned here.

As with Janice, mindfulness of changes in body states, for example, heart rate and stomach sensations, can be useful. You might also check for shifts anywhere in your body.

- Sight—note any changes in your visual perception (focus, sharpness, coloration).
- Hearing—pay attention to possible variation in how you perceive the sounds around you (louder, softer, clearer, faded).
- Muscle tone—are there shifts in tension or looseness anywhere in your body?
- Breathing—notice where your air goes as well as the depth of your breaths.
- Temperature—you may get warmer or cooler, either all over or in particular places, for example, hands going cold or face feeling hot.
- Miscellaneous sensations—for example, prickles or pressure that come and go.

Please note: if focusing on body sensations is distressing for you, makes you anxious, or causes dissociation, use other aspects of mindfulness (below) to find your gauge.

Remember to consider the other foundations of mindfulness: feelings, thoughts, and images. You might find or discover a particular image in your mind's eye that fluctuates (remember Janet's rabbit). It could also be a sound image, like a song or poem that goes through your head. You might also pay attention to changes in your mood or your thoughts. Unfortunately, it would be impossible to give you a complete list. So be open to the possibility that your gauge will be something different than I have written about here. The most important thing is that you discover what *your* gauge is and identify what changes in your gauge signify for you.

It is always best to begin exercising new tools with tasks and situations where there is no risk. You could explore some of the same things as Janice: choosing what you wear, eat, or watch on television. Do not be surprised if you find you have a different gauge for different types of choices. For example, perhaps it is stomach sensations that are the strongest when you decide what to eat, but it is your mood that is affected most when you decide what you will wear.

The exercises that follow are meant to help you to find and practice with your own gauges. Do not become discouraged if you sometimes forget to use your gauge or cannot access it. Any new skill gets easier and more habitual with use. The more you can practice when you are feeling calm, the more available your gauge will be to you in situations where you are ill at ease.

NOTE: The following exercises may be done with eyes open or eyes closed. If you are not sure, alternate and see what works best for you.

Exercise 1: The Foundations of Mindfulness

What is the best gauge for you? Do you fare best when you pay attention to your:

- Body sensations
- Moods
- Feelings
- Thoughts
- Your mind's images

If you already know, you might want to skip these exercises. For those of you who do not know your best gauge, experimenting with each is the way to find out.

Choose one of the gauge categories above (e.g., sensations, feelings), then try one or more of these mindful experiments:

- Imagine having something warm to drink. Notice what changes in the gauge.
- Imagine drinking something cold. Notice what changes in the gauge.

- Take time to decide which chair to sit in, imagining first and then trying two or more possibilities. Notice what changes in the gauge. Is it different when you actually sit than when you just imagine sitting?
- Next time you are hungry, select two alternatives (e.g., an apple or an orange). Before you take a bite, imagine eating one and see if there are any fluctuations in the gauge. Then try the same with the other option. Pay attention to which you end up eating and identify the basis of your decision. Notice if your actual reaction is the same or different than you predicted.

After you try one gauge option (e.g., your mood), you can go on to another (e.g., body sensations), and so on. But do not overwhelm yourself by attempting too much at once. It is fine to try one and later return to this exercise to try something else. Eventually it would be good to try them all, or to create your own experiments. Do not forget to include and keep track of any other gauges you discover on your own.

Your most reliable gauges will be those that are easy for you to identify and have clearly noticeable changes. For instance, if your heart rate always goes up as an adverse reaction and down as a pleasant reaction, or if you always hear the same (or same type of) tune when you are doing or eating something that feels good and another when you are doing or eating something that does not feel good, then those will be reliable. The only way to discover your gauges is to experiment with many possibilities. It is worth the trouble, because when you have the use of one or more, they will serve you well.

Exercise 2: Practice Your Gauges With Benign Choices

For testing your newfound gauges, start with choices that have little to no risk associated with them. For example: Which cereal for breakfast? Should you wear a coat or sweater today? To apply your gauge, take an extra couple of seconds to consider or imagine whatever the choice is. Then notice how your gauge changes to help guide your final decision.

You could also experiment with all types of foods, using mindfulness to monitor how you react to different choices. Notice which foods help you to feel calmer or if any make you feel more stimulated or hyped up. Reactions to food are very, very individual. For instance, some people feel very calm after eating an apple or a potato and others (such as Barry) anxious (of course, many notice nothing at all). Applying mindfulness to what you eat can be a good way to discover which foods might be allies in your trauma recovery.

As you pay more and more attention, it is possible that you will discover additional gauges based in somatic markers that were previously outside of your awareness. Do not be disappointed if this does not happen, as you can rest assured that your somatic markers are working anyway. However, if any do emerge, take note.

Exercise 3: Practice Your Gauges With More Relevant Choices

Once you feel you have gained some proficiency with your gauges in benign situations, you can test them with something more difficult. This is what Janice did when she used her gauge to help her determine a kind of touch that she might tolerate. Remember, she first imagined several scenarios and then picked one to try based on which image gave her the most comfortable response.

Pick something in your daily life that has a little more risk to it (but not the most risky, yet) and imagine several possibilities. Perhaps it will be something you want to buy, or deciding which friend to invite for dinner. Use your gauge to pick the choice you will pursue. After you have followed through, evaluate how accurate your gauge was. If you were successful, then you can try an even riskier situation. However, if the result did not go as hoped, review your steps and see if there was something in your gauge that you missed—or if you need a different gauge for that kind of choice—before going on to something more difficult.

Exercise 4: Practice Your Gauges to Plot Your Course

When you are ready, you can apply your gauge to decide your next step or to make a decision about a strategy, exercise, or direction for your recovery. Turn to the table of contents and take a moment to contemplate each of the other keys. See which one gives you the most positive response in your gauge. It may be the next chapter or it may be the last. Though it might be a good idea to read or skim the book through first, you do not have to apply the chapters in order. Take them in turn as they feel right to you, using your gauge as a guide. That means you may put off topics or exercises that feel daunting and start with the ones that feel the most comfortable. It may be that you skip one or more altogether. In doing so, you will be guiding yourself toward your safest trauma recovery. One caveat: If you decide to read the chapters out of order, you will periodically come to a reference to an earlier chapter. I will endeavor to include a page reference so you can review the relevant excerpt.

Evaluate This Key

At the beginning of this chapter, I expressed the hope that you will be able to use one or more mindfulness gauges to evaluate and plan the safest recovery program for your unique needs and situation. Now is a good time to start.

Take a few minutes to review the exercises you have done

thus far and pay attention to your gauge. Which results lean in a positive direction? Which in a negative direction? Based on your evaluation, which exercises or strategies would you repeat and which would you not? Will the results of your evaluation affect how you choose other exercises in this book? If so, how?

Plan How to (or Not to) Use This Key

Is this key for you? If so, why? If not, why not? Consider if you will use this key in the future. In which kinds of situations or with which sorts of dilemmas will you find this key most useful?

It is common to become enthusiastic about new tools but then sometimes lose connection to them or forget about them—I certainly know this tendency in myself and others in both my personal and professional spheres. If you have found using your mindful gauge of benefit, plan how you will remember to apply it when it could be of use. For example, you could post a note on your bathroom mirror, draw a symbol on the palm of your hand, or leave yourself a voice mail message. It does not matter what strategy you use to remember your gauge, just that you have one that will jog your memory and help you to keep using your gauge where appropriate and helpful.

Endnote: Mindfulness and Common Sense

I am often asked, "How will I know if it is mindfulness telling me 'no' or if I am just afraid or resisting?" My answer might surprise you. Actually, I do not think the difference matters. Any time your system is strongly telling you no, there must be a good reason. For an important decision, mindfulness should be a major contributor, but not always the only factor. In general, it should be joined by available knowledge and liberal amounts of common sense. Sometimes it will be primarily mindfulness; at other times it will be common sense, which carries the most weight. What follows is a personal example of the cooperation between mindfulness, knowledge, and common sense.

Shortly before my 51st birthday, I came down with acute appendicitis. The diagnosis was confirmed in the emergency room late one night and I was scheduled for surgery early the next morning. I had never had surgery before and while I waited, I was terrified. Every one of my mindful gauges screamed that I did not want to have the operation. On the other hand, everything in my common sense told me that, though afraid, I must go along with the doctor's recommendation. There was no doubt that my mindful reluctance had good reason: All surgery carries risk. Still, my common sense, supported by my basic knowledge concerning the consequences of untreated appendicitis, convinced me that surgery was my best option. However, that did not mean ignoring my mindful gauges. I actually paid a lot of attention to my internal screaming and was able to talk with the emergency room doctor, the surgeon, and even the anesthesiologist about my concerns and fears. The support and respect that they then showed for my feelings (not to mention their competence) helped to make that potentially traumatic situation manageable as well as successful. The professionals deserve a large share of the credit, but so do I— for paying attention to both my common sense *and* mindfulness.

BEGIN WITH YOUR EPILOGUE . . . YOU MADE IT!

What does not destroy me, makes me stronger. —NIETZSCHE

Misperception—in body and mind—that past trauma is still happening is the main feature that distinguishes PTSD. In this chapter I will help you understand what is going on in your brain when you feel as though your past trauma continues. This chapter will enable you to realize the true conclusion to your traumatic situation: You survived. You will also learn to pay attention to the internal and external factors that have and do continue to contribute to your ongoing survival.

The Issue

How often do you recount the story of your trauma, to yourself or to others? Do you feel better when you describe the details or does the telling leave you feeling disconnected or more shaken? Maybe you do not really or completely remember what happened but you are trying to piece it together, trying to jog your brain to tell you why you continue to be so upset.

Typically, when relating a trauma, you start at the beginning of the account. The therapist or friend says, "Tell me what happened." The self-help book instructs you to write down all the details. Too often, you can get stuck at the beginning or in the middle, and rarely, if ever, get to the end—the actual end. You may get as far as when you got away, the earthquake stopped, the perpetrator lost interest, or the ambulance arrived. But that is not the actual end. The true conclusion to any trauma is the arrival at now, today. Getting to now is the testament that you made it, you are here. Whatever it was, you survived it. For that reason, this is the place I find it best to start trauma recovery—with the epilogue, the fact that *you made it*.

The physical indicators of trauma and PTSD include hyperarousal (e.g., hypervigilance, hyper startle response), intrusive memories, sleep and eating disturbances, and concentration difficulties. Whether someone qualifies for the diagnosis of PTSD or something else depends, in part, on the level of these disturbances, how much they impact and interfere with the person's daily life. All of these somatic symptoms have something very important in common: They are the result of a nervous system that continues to behave as if the traumatic event is about to occur again. That is why it may not feel like your trauma is over even though it actually is. Peter Levine, in his book *Waking the Tiger*, describes how:

- The physical sensations of trauma continue to activate the mind's fear response,
- which in turn activates the physical response to danger,
- which is the root of the physical sensations of trauma.

It is a vicious loop. When you are in that cycle, your mind and body persist in behaving as if the trauma continues to occur or keeps happening over and over again. A key element of breaking this cycle involves updating the mind to recognize that the trauma concluded and that the event lies in the past. Beginning with your epilogue can help toward that end.

Whether you are going to process all of the memory of your trauma or not (discussed in Key 3), beginning with the epilogue will make either option more manageable. Gaining confidence about the end point of your trauma and the fact of your survival can make dealing with additional aspects much easier. Though the occasions are extremely rare, I have even seen this simple concept, when thoroughly digested, be all that was needed to heal someone's trauma. Of course, for such "miracle cures," timing and other factors must be factored in. Nonetheless, focusing on the epilogue can be a powerful ally and key to safe trauma recovery.

The following example will help to clarify the potential of starting with the epilogue to your trauma. It will illustrate how creating an epilogue can enable your mind and body to recognize and accept that you survived.

Stephanie, Stuck in the Past

At 42, Stephanie was terrified to sit in her backyard. It was beautifully landscaped and her gardener kept it in great shape. But she could not make use of it herself. If she wanted to be relaxed and enjoy the beauty and peacefulness of the garden, she had to do it from inside the house. She would often sit in the family room, her eyes drinking in the mix of colors and the movement of birds and butterflies. On weekends she would watch her children from a distance as they played on the grass, wreaked havoc in the flowerbeds, and had water fights with the hose. During family barbecues she would find any excuse to stay inside: Preparing salads, scooping ice cream, doing the dishes, ducking inside while complaining it was too hot or too cold or too windy. Everybody knew why, so no one tried to force her to stay outdoors. Her husband and kids wished they could help her, but they had long ago given up trying.

When she was 11, Stephanie was attacked by a swarm of angry wasps. Her father doused her with water and pulled her to safety but could not calm her panic. Even at the hospital she kept crying, "I can't get away! Get me away! I can't get away!" The emergency room doctor treated her many stings and prescribed a sedative to calm her hysteria. Nonetheless, for the next 30-plus years, Stephanie avoided lawns, trees, and flowers—anything that could attract a bee or wasp—at all costs.

When she first came to see me, Stephanie admitted it was at the urging of her family. Her husband finally pushed her to get some help, insisting "It's about time!" Though sent by her family, Stephanie did agree it was a good idea since she longed to join them on the patio. We discussed the pros and cons of dealing with the wasp issue. It was not a question of whether or not to remember what happened—she was doing that on a regular basis. It was her anxiety that was crippling her, gripping her just about any time she stepped out of doors, especially any area with plant life and the potential for flying insects—as is most of the landscape in Southern California. Sometimes she had panic attacks or full-blown flashbacks. On the occasions when she would totally panic, she would collapse and cover her head while repeatedly crying, "I can't get away."

Apply a Little Theory

Stephanie's difficulty is typical of trauma: A part of her is still bound to the past, in that single, horrific scene when she was 11 years old. Otherwise, Stephanie functioned normally. So why was she not able to go outside?

One answer may be found in the brain, in understanding how memory functions differently during and following highly stressful events. Bear with me while I explain a little neuroscience.

There are two structures in the midbrain, also known as the *limbic system,* that have special roles in remembering: the *amygdala* and the *hippocampus.* Understanding their function will help to explain what went wrong in Stephanie's memory, why she continued to be afraid to go outside. That, in turn, will help to shed light on what might help her—and hopefully also you. To simplify the discussion, I will be referring to these and other brain structures as separate entities. However, it is important to note that no part of the brain (or the body, for that matter) works on its own.

The amygdala directs the brain's emotional response system. It tells you how to react to any situation, usually before you have any conscious thought involved. Keeping track of all of the pleasant and unpleasant experiences in your life via somatic markers is a major part of the amygdala's job. It remembers the *feel* of those events, not the facts. Your instant smile and warm sensation around your heart when you hear the voice of someone you love on the other end of the phone — even before you have remembered the person's name — is an example of the amygdala at work. As you may have guessed, the amygdala is central in recording and reactivating somatic markers (see Key 1).

The other brain area, the hippocampus, remembers facts but not emotions, such as the name of the person at the other end of the phone, and when or where something happened. It records the time frame of significant events, the start, the middle, and the end. When needed, it sends these facts on to the cortex, the thinking part of the brain, the structure responsible for conscious thought. However, often during trauma, ultra-high levels of stress hormones — necessary for the survival responses of flight, fight, or freeze — stop the hippocampus from functioning properly. When that happens, an accurate time frame of events does not get logged. The event might be remembered, but in jumbled order or with significantly missing steps. Typical in trauma, without the hippocampus able to carry out its role, it may not register that the trauma actually ended. PTSD is often the result of just such a hippocampal failure.

That is what I suspected was happening with Stephanie. She was so overwhelmed when attacked by the swarm that her hippocampus went "off-line." Then, as an adult, when she had a panic attack or a flashback, she really felt as if she was again being attacked by the wasps. She even cried the same words she did then: "I can't get away!" During these episodes, her adrenaline level would skyrocket as it had back then, again preventing the hippocampus from doing its job. This kind of memory disturbance is very typical in people who are still suffering from a past traumatic event, even if, like Stephanie, they are not debilitated enough to qualify for a diagnosis of PTSD. Their bodies and minds have not figured out that their traumatic event actually came to an end and they survived it. To make it possible to separate that past event from the present time, the hippocampus must be helped to work properly again. It must be able to tell the cortex when that event actually happened—in the past—and that it is not happening now. Every one of this book's eight keys aim to contribute to better hippocampal function. The one that follows is the most directly targeted toward that goal. It is the key that released the lock that bound Stephanie to her past. It has potential to do the same for you.

Discovering the Key

Stephanie and I discussed the theory (similar to what is written in the section above). She figured that her thinking brain, her cortex, had not yet grasped that she survived the wasps. In addition, she was concerned that her fear of being outdoors had actually become a phobia. We considered alternative strategies and methods with regard to her goal: Stephanie wanted to slowly build her tolerance to being outside, a small step at a time—a popular approach for dealing with phobias, including those with roots in a trauma. She asked me to accompany her to a park. Before proceeding, we outlined steps that would challenge her wasp fears gradually. First, we just sat in her car on the edge of the park. Next, we walked around the perimeter on the sidewalk. Both of those steps went fairly easily. Stephanie was a bit nervous at the beginning of each of the challenges, but relaxed by the time we returned to my office. However, on our third

excursion to the park, we walked onto the edge of the grass and
disaster struck.

A single bee, not even a wasp, flew quickly past our heads.
Stephanie heard the buzz and glimpsed it out of the corner of
her eye. In the same way as she had described to me, she instantly fell to the ground, covered her head, and started screaming, "I can't get away!"

For a few seconds I held back, evaluating her situation.
Then I knelt down beside her and said in a firm voice, "Stephanie, you *did* get away!" I was aiming to use my cortex and hippocampus to communicate to and strengthen hers. I had to get
a little louder and say it several times to get her attention, but
eventually she stopped yelling. Still panicked, she looked at
me. I repeated, "You got away. You did get away!" I could see
in her eyes that she was trying to make sense of where she was
and what I was saying. I repeated the same words a few more
times until the confusion in her eyes cleared a little. Then I
ventured a bit further: "I actually know that you got away. I am
very sure about that."

"You're sure?" she asked in a small, slightly skeptical voice.

"Quite sure. Absolutely sure." By this time we were sitting
facing each other on the grass. "Would you like me to tell you
how I am so sure . . . or can you figure it out?"

Stephanie thought for a moment. She looked around. Then
realization dawned. Her eyes wide, she looked a little like a kid
who had figured out the test answer after a long struggle. "Oh!
I must have gotten away. I'm *here*. Is that what you mean?"

"Yes, you are here." I smiled and pointed toward the ground
and around at the park. "Because you are here with me."

I asked her to identify the park and her current age, which
she was able to do. "We are in a city park and I am 42." Then
she added, "I could not be here with you now if I had not gotten away from the wasps back then." She started to cry. Not the
fearful crying from before, but sobs of relief.

Thinking over what had happened, I got an idea. The next
week I suggested that she write an epilogue to the story of the

wasp attack. I wanted her to record all sorts of events—happy and sad, challenging and successful—that had taken place since. If my idea was correct, it would help her hippocampus to place the wasp memory among the other events in her history. She completed her written epilogue a month later. It included an extensive list. Many years had passed since that attack and the epilogue confirmed that she had gotten away a long time ago. This key made a major contribution toward Stephanie's recovery from the wasp attack and helped her to participate in her family life in the outdoors. She would repeat the same principles when she became nervous at the sight or sound of a bee or wasp, reminding herself, "I did get away, because I am here." Additional keys were also helpful for her. (For more on Stephanie's recovery, see Key 4.)

Applications for You

Following the success of my work with Stephanie, I began to apply the same principles with other clients. I would also suggest the idea to individuals calling for personal consultation and to professionals in my classes to apply with their clients. The feedback from most of them has been extremely positive. For those who are struggling with trauma memories, writing their epilogue appears to help them to stay anchored in the present while remembering the past. Generally, identifying the epilogue reduces the terror of the trauma memory because it confirms the actual outcome. In addition, creating the epilogue makes possible a separation of past from present that previously appeared to be unavailable.

One of the characteristics of trauma is the strong pull of the traumatic memory. You may feel as though the trauma continues to happen or happens again. It may be that you suffer intrusions (flashbacks) that remind you of your trauma—associated reactions in your body or visual, sound, or smell images in your mind—and have a destabilizing impact on your daily life. If traumatic memory is weighing you down so much that your ability to function and be engaged in your life is compromised, you may be suffering from PTSD. However, like Stephanie, many people experience trauma while continuing to manage, more or less. Whichever category you fit into, recognizing the fact that you survived your trauma could help you.

Stephanie's story demonstrates one of the keys to trauma recovery: recognizing survival, *because you are here*. Of course, that fact does not always sink in so quickly as it did for Stephanie that day in the park. And like Stephanie, it may not be the only necessary step (see Key 4). But living and dealing with your past trauma will become easier if you help yourself to grasp that simple truth.

The same applies for you as for Stephanie. Whether you have experienced a car accident, earthquake, child abuse, rape, terrorist bombing—whatever—the fact that you are holding this book in your hand and reading these words means you survived it. So you, too, can help your hippocampus by focusing on your epilogue. When your hippocampus functions properly again, it will be able to tell your amygdala that it can stop acting (and reacting) as if the trauma repeats or continues.

Writing your epilogue may be all you need. For some people, writing the epilogue will etch into their mind and body the fact that they survived. If that happens for you, you may not need to do more. Writing your epilogue may also be appropriate for those of you who do not want or are not ready to go over your memories, or those of you who feel worse from dealing with memories. In addition, if you are one who does or will benefit from processing your memories, writing your epilogue first will make dealing with the trauma details much easier. You will have already reinforced your survival, and that will help you to keep one foot firmly in the now as you deal with the past.

Is Beginning With My Epilogue for Me?

If you sometimes (or all the time) feel as though your trauma is still happening or happening again, then the exercises below may be helpful for you. However, they will only be a good idea if your traumatic incidents have actually ended—in real time. This will be obvious for most of you. But due to the effect of trauma on the brain discussed in the theory section, you could be in doubt. A calendar will be an ally in such a case. A spread of weeks, months, or years between the incident and now would likely indicate the trauma is actually over. Exceptions would include, for example, if you are still recovering from physical injuries, a court case is pending, or you have yet to find replacement housing.

Another category of exception will involve any of you who continue to live with or in trauma on a daily basis. This group includes victims of domestic violence who are still in danger from the abuser or someone living in a war-torn country. In these and similar situations, trauma has not ended; it is ongoing. If your circumstances fit into this category, the exercises below may not be useful for you. However, you might discover you are able to adapt one or more to your own needs.

There is a final consideration before trying any of the exercises below, and actually all of the exercises in the previous and subsequent chapters. Do not attempt any that do not make sense to you or do not feel right. Use and listen to your mindful gauge in choosing what you do and do not attempt.

Exercise 1: Your New Mantra

Which words will help you to remember that you survived? You might begin with Stephanie's "I know I survived because I am here," then edit to make the phrase your own. Maintain the essence of the message but use words that speak clearly to you. Stephanie found that repeating the sentence while looking around and noticing things in her environment helped. Sometimes she would add, "because I am now 42," or "because I have two daughters." Being specific will strengthen the message.

Write down several possibilities and then use the mindful gauge you developed from the first key to help you to zero in on the best sentence or phrase for you. The correct combination might come to you very quickly or might take some time. It is also possible that what is best might vary from one day to the next. Be patient and let your gauge guide you.

Exercise 2: Write Your Own Epilogue

Would you like to write your epilogue? You can do so a little at a time and see how it goes for you. There are many ways to approach the creation of an epilogue. It usually works best to start with now and work backward. But if that is not right for you, begin with a time after the trauma and work forward. Some people write full sentences, as in a narrative or story; others jot down a simple outline or list. It is most important to include the events that will remind you that you actually survived your trauma. For example, an adult writing an epilogue for a teen trauma might include high school graduation, entering college, or earning a degree. Make sure to include your present day, highlighting anything that will reinforce the time difference between the trauma and now, such as what you do, who you live with, or how old you are.

Whether the time span since your trauma is short or long, including today's details is especially important. Listing material objects can be useful to the epilogue to emphasize that time has passed since your trauma. Technology, such as an up-to-date computer or mobile phone, is particularly useful for this purpose. If you buy something new, you can also add the new item to your epilogue: "I bought _____ to remind myself that I survived."

Exercise 3: Celebrate Your Survival

Plan and carry out a ritual of some sort that recognizes and marks the truth of your survival. Some people think they have to wait until they have cleared up all of the issues of their trauma before they can do this. Not so. At any time, you can acknowledge that you survived. You can do this on your own or in the company of others. And, in fact, you can celebrate survival as many times as you wish. Buy a gift, make a special meal, conduct a ceremony, create a piece of art—anything that meets the goal. Whatever you decide to do, use your imagination and creativity to find or design something that reinforces your survival.

I did exactly that for myself years ago. I decided I wanted a Purple Heart, like the medal given to injured soldiers, because I felt as though I had been through a kind of war myself. I saw one or two in antique stores but eventually decided that the actual soldier's medal was not really appropriate. Sadly, I shelved the idea. However, a short time later, in a small boutique, I found the perfect substitute: a small, inexpensive, wooden pin in the shape of a heart and painted purple with tiny accenting colored flowers. It was beautiful and perfect. I was very emotional as I bought it and carried it from the shop. For me that little purple heart (which I still have) symbolized my survival and was part of an evolving kindness and compassion toward myself. The heart itself was important, but equally significant was that I wanted to give myself such a gift and would make the effort to find it.

Evaluate This Key

Refer back to the mindful gauge you adopted in the first key. What happens with that gauge when you use your mantra, think about your epilogue, reward yourself, or plan your survival celebration? Does your gauge tell you this is something good for you right now, or does it tell you to put one or more of the exercises aside until later? What does your common sense say about it?

Try only one exercise at a time. Breaking each down into manageable bits will make it easier to evaluate along the way. Stop periodically and evaluate how you feel. Remember you do not have to do any exercise all at once, or at all. You can do a little, then take a break before you go further.

Plan How to (or Not to) Use This Key

How often would it be good for you to reinforce your epilogue, that you survived? Try different intervals and see what is optimal for you. Some people do this daily, perhaps when they wake up or on their way to bed. Others remind themselves several times a day. Try variations to find what works best for you.

Endnote: Special Situations

It actually does not matter if you remember your trauma at all to take advantage of this key. Your now is your now. In fact, starting at the end, with the epilogue, is one great strategy for those of you who are frustrated because you do not remember what happened in the past. You do not need to worry. No matter what happened to you in the past, your epilogue is totally visible today. You can see it right now where you are and what you are doing. Start there. The next key will also help you in understanding that trauma memory is not necessary for trauma recovery.

KEY 3

REMEMBERING IS *NOT* REQUIRED

Don't let your past dictate who you are, but let it be part of who you will become.

—NICK to TULA, *My Big Fat Greek Wedding* (2002)

It is always a good idea to learn from the past, but not always to dwell on it. Processing trauma memories is a common practice in trauma therapy and is often advised in self-help books. However, there is a growing debate in the field of traumatic stress: How useful is the revisiting of trauma memories? The jury is still out. As common sense would predict, it seems to be an individual matter—helpful for some but not for others. A good many benefit from going over their traumas, sometimes repeatedly. On the other hand, some become further disabled by the practice. Actually, most people recover from trauma without any formalized reviewing of the past at all. It is a viable option, though not necessary nor even always advisable.

This chapter is not concerned with whether or not you remember your trauma(s); safe recovery is possible in either instance. The subject matter of these next pages involves illuminating commonsense options for deciding if, when, and how much to work with trauma memory. At the time I was pursuing my own trauma recovery, there was only one acceptable option. The only philosophy at the time assumed that traumatic memories must be recovered and processed. I remember sometimes wishing there were other choices. Since then, I am happy to say, the field of traumatic stress has matured and more options have emerged.

Dr. Pierre Janet's Key

The clearest, most commonsense framework for managing trauma memory actually evolved in the late 1800s. I am hoping that eventually it will be the standard for all systems and methods of trauma recovery. In the latter part of the 19th century, Dr. Pierre Janet laid a firm foundation for the future of trauma recovery. He defined a three-pronged system for healing from past trauma. His *phase-oriented approach* can be applied across the full spectrum of available philosophies, methods, and models. However, to my knowledge, the only previous discussion of Janet's concepts in the self-help genre appears in Judith Herman's seminal classic, *Trauma and Recovery.*

- *Phase I* is concerned with establishing safety and stabilization—whether that takes hours, weeks, or even years.
- *Phase II* involves processing trauma memories.
- *Phase III* focuses on integration, applying what was gained from Phases I and II into the mainstream of daily life.

According to Janet, it is not advisable to move to Phase II, working with past trauma, until the goals of Phase I are achieved, that is, until the traumatized individual is safe, stable, and able to function on a daily basis. I could not agree with Janet's philosophy more and have never encountered a trauma client, professional, or author who disagreed with Janet *in principle.* However, there are few who actually follow his framework. Most clients as well as authors and practitioners seem to become too impatient to get at the trauma memories, sometimes with disastrous results. Waiting to ensure stability seems much too difficult for many.

Janet's model is full of common sense. You may have noticed by now, dealing with your own issues, that recalling trauma—even under the best of circumstances—throws you off balance. For anyone, recalling a traumatic past *in an already wobbly state* only increases the wobble. Of course, many people can manage moderate levels of unsteadiness. But for those who live with emotional instability on a daily basis due to their trauma, increasing that instability can land them in deeper trouble. The concern here involves the necessity of maintaining an adequate level of functioning on a daily basis. This is quite different from becoming upset, which is a normal part of life in general, and trauma recovery in particular. However, if you are not able to continue to function—to think clearly and care for yourself, in spite of being upset—that is cause for concern. Janet's model, which requires stability (able to function, but not without feelings) before approaching potentially destabilizing memories, ensures safety and makes infinite sense. However, for some there is this risk: If you prioritize stabilization before dealing with the past, you may find that you must put off moving on to focusing on your trauma memories—which is not necessarily a bad thing. For some of you that would be a relief. For others, postponing or even skipping delving into your memories will be a scary idea, perhaps even seeming intolerable.

Take a minute or two to consider your actual goal: Is it to process and reprocess your past, or is it to better your future? For many of you, the surest route to the latter will be via memory processing. However, for others, the better future will be found via a memory bypass. When remembering trauma interferes with your quality of life, then consider if avoiding memory might serve you better—at least for a while.

The first goal of trauma recovery should and must be to *improve your quality of life* on a daily basis. Contrary to common sense, however, processing trauma memory is and always has been the primary goal of trauma self-help books and therapies. While some individuals definitely do benefit from revisiting their traumatic situations, all too many do not. In fact, a significant portion of individuals either do not want to remember (see Stuart in the next section), cannot remember (like Martha, mentioned in Key 1), or become decidedly worse when they do remember (like Stephanie in the previous chapter). In any of these instances, remembering should never be required by you or anyone else.

Of course, working with your trauma memories might be an important part of bettering your daily life. In such a case, moving on to that task after you are sure you can manage it (when you are stable) will be logical for you. However, you may already know the opposite is true for you: remembering trauma makes it more difficult for you to function, including accomplishing simple tasks, or enjoying the company of others. In that circumstance, reviewing your trauma will not be a good idea in the short or perhaps even the long term.

The theory and exercises associated with Key 3 will help you to identify your unique needs and capacities for remembering trauma. By the chapter's end, you will be better able to judge for yourself whether you should, now or later, or at all:

- Tackle your memories in detail
- Review them in general
- Leave them alone entirely
- Table this decision until a later time

Please remember: They are your memories and you have a choice whether or not you want to spend time on them. Being able to predict if you are someone who could benefit from processing the memory of your trauma or if you would be better off—at least for now—leaving your memories alone could help you to make an informed choice. In a few pages I will outline criteria for that purpose. However, first I would like to show you an example of what recovery from trauma without processing memories of the event might look like.

An Example of Recovery in Phase I: Stuart

Stuart began having periodic flashbacks and frequent panic attacks following his survival of a terrorist bombing. I first met him several years following the incident, after he had tried medication and psychotherapy to no avail.

In discussion of his goals, Stuart was clear: He wanted to be free of the panic. However, remembering the details of the bombing was still so upsetting that he feared to go there at all. Respectful of his wishes, I suggested we could possibly tackle his panic attacks by investigating their course. If we could identify a pattern, we might, I proposed, be able to find a way to interrupt it. For that to have a chance, though, Stuart would have to be willing to take on regular homework assignments. He was agreeable to that.

At our second meeting, I proposed to Stuart that he take the role of a scientist. I suggest this often, as it is a great way to get people fully engaged in their recovery process. Moreover, the information they gather can be invaluable for helping themselves. The first step involved mindfulness (per Key 1). Stuart learned to pay attention to his body sensations, emotions, thoughts, and feelings. I suggested that he get in the habit of observing the shifts in those states as much as possible for a week or two. As he became more adept, I added the next step: keeping track of what he ate and drank, what he read or watched on television, the topic of conversations with friends and family, and so on, and how each affected his body sensations, emotions, thoughts, and feelings. Of particular interest would be his state immediately before the onset of panic, and anything he could identify that was different on the days he had a panic attack from the days he did not.

Soon, we could identify several patterns from Stuart's research. Certain types of music helped him to feel calmer, while other ones made him more agitated. He found that eating chicken and steak made him feel more present and stable but desserts, except for ice cream, had the opposite effect. Most important, Stuart eventually identified that every panic attack he had was preceded by one or more cups of coffee within 30–60 minutes before the onset of the attack. As he paid more attention, he observed that during the first half hour after drinking coffee, his heart rate would climb. He would notice he was nervous, then anxious. Finally, if his heart rate did not quickly decrease, he would break out in a cold sweat, feel faint, and begin to panic in earnest. The attack would last around an hour and subside in sync with a reduction in heart rate as the caffeine worked its way through (and out of) his system.

Because of the cold sweat and fainting feeling, I asked Stuart to get a physical examination and a stress test. I wanted to make sure there was no biological cause, complication, or connection, and no heart irregularity. However, all exams and tests were negative. His doctor confirmed Stuart's symptoms were provoked by caffeine.

That was a tough realization for Stuart. He loved coffee and the social aspects of drinking it with his colleagues and friends. He had always been skeptical of "the herbal tea crowd" and was loath to join them. However, after trying a single coffee-free (and other caffeinated beverage-free) week he felt so much better that he was willing to make the switch permanently. When he held to caffeine abstinence, he was entirely free of panic attacks.

Stuart recalled that he had been drinking espresso at a café at the time of the bombing. It is likely his heart rate was already high and the fright of the bombing spiked it higher. Thereafter, the coffee taste combined with the increased heart rate became associated with the bombing and mortal danger, triggering his subsequent panic attacks.

Many would not consider Stuart's increased control over his symptoms to be a cure. And Stuart knew that the actual bomb attack still played a big role in his (much reduced) anxiety. But the quality of his life improved a great deal. Moreover, he was very happy to feel mastery over his body and appreciated that he had not been forced to delve into recollections that he feared would be overwhelming. We parted company with the understanding that my door would remain open to him should he be interested in or require further help.

What works varies widely as individuals are so different from each other. But the Phase I (stability) principles applied in Stuart's case, along with others discussed in this book and elsewhere, can be used by most anyone. The success of concentrated work on stabilization demonstrates that processing trauma memories is not necessary for improving quality of life. It is an option you can choose or not based on what you decide is most likely to benefit you. For many survivors of trauma, the successful self-control achieved by Stuart would be welcomed as a huge step. For some it would even be considered a cure. However, there is one more step to add before calling Stuart's improvement a successful recovery.

Oft-Neglected Phase III

A common pitfall of trauma recovery is neglecting Phase III, integration. Most of the time people get so involved in stabilization (Phase I) or the intrigue or destabilization of remembering trauma (Phase II) that integration (Phase III) becomes all but forgotten. While Janet advised that integration should be the endnote to trauma recovery, I propose an alternative view. It is my recommendation that integration is best woven throughout the recovery process. Whether emphasizing stabilization or trauma memories, integration should always be alongside. That way any result or change along the way can be relevantly integrated into daily life. For example, Stuart had to learn how to take his new knowledge about caffeine and the change in his behavior (no longer being a coffee drinker), and apply it on a daily basis. This involved not only a dietary concern, but also dealing with his family, colleagues, and friends who would be surprised or remark about his change of taste or habit. We took time to discuss how he was adjusting and where it was easy or difficult. For example, he sometimes rehearsed how to respond to a confrontation or smart remark. Integration for you might mean talking with your partner or best friend about the changes you are making or keeping a log or diary to help you make sense of your changing reactions, view, or situation.

Which Phase Is for Me?

How do you know if you would be best off focusing on Phase I stabilization or the memory processing of Phase II? First and foremost, you need to make an honest evaluation of your current level of stability and safety. Below is a list of general considerations. Please feel free to add any points that are missing which apply to your unique situation. Some of the essentials necessary for stability:

- You have access to adequate amounts of the basics needed for daily life: shelter, food, clothing, companionship.
- You control your memories and symptoms; they do not control you. This includes your being able to calm yourself or stop a flashback (see Key 4).
- You are able to manage a normal day, whatever is normal for you and your role in your culture, family, and job. This includes a normal schedule and activities.

Basic safety implies that you are not continuing to live under threat of trauma. For example:

- If you suffered an accident, the cause has been completely repaired or replaced (e.g., stairwell, automobile).

- If you are a refugee, you have been granted legal residence in your new country.
- If you are a victim of violence, all of the physical injuries are healed and the legal procedures are concluded. Either the perpetrator is incarcerated or deceased, or your living situation is secret or adequately protected by distance, locks, guard dog, and so on.
- If you have been a victim of domestic violence, you are no longer living with the abuser, or the abuser has stopped abusing and you are getting (or have had) couples or family counseling.
- If you were abused as a child, you are no longer living with or near the abuser nor in an abusive relationship.

Of course the examples above do not cover all possibilities but should give you an idea of what is meant by safety. If you are not currently safe, that must be your first priority.

Before Moving on to Memories (Phase II)

If you meet the stabilization criteria for Phase I, there are still several things to consider before moving on to Phase II.

1. Do you want to revisit your traumatic memories?
2. When you pay attention to the past, do you lose connection with your present life?
3. Some people become decidedly worse from attention to their past.

Do You Want to Revisit Your Traumatic Memories?

This may seem an absurd question, but actually it is very, very important. There is no reason to revisit your past if you do not want to or if you do not see a value in doing so. Do not let any doctor, author, therapist, family member, or friend push or force you into reviewing the past. Giving in to another's pressure in this regard could land you in a much worse condition. However, this is probably easier said than done for many. I was coming unglued before I could convince my therapist to change direction or back off. So I do understand it is not a simple matter to tell a close relation or an authority figure—especially a doctor or therapist—no. You might need support to assert your right to choose. If possible, discussing and rehearsing with a friend who is not pressuring you might prove very helpful. Ultimately, it would be best for you to find your own way to phrase what you want to say. However, below I include a sampling of ways to phrase a refusal, listed here for inspiration and just to get you started.

- When I have tried what you ask, I feel worse (or have a bad week), so I do not want to do it again, at least for a while.
- No, that does not feel right for me.
- Sorry, that does not make sense for me.
- You are going to have to trust me to know myself and what I need.
- I appreciate your input and am sorry we disagree. But even if I could be making a mistake, I need to try it this way first.

You are also welcome to share this chapter (or entire book) with anyone who is insistent.

When You Pay Attention to the Past, Do You Lose Connection With Your Present Life?

Some trauma victims become so absorbed by focusing on the past that they miss their life now. Trauma memory processing should be a sideline, like using physical therapy or exercise to heal a physical injury. It should never be the main preoccupa-

tion. If you find you cannot live your daily life while focusing on
the past, then consider putting your memories aside, at least
until you are able to manage a better balance. For some of you
this advice will come as a blessed relief. Others may be rolling
your eyes and saying, "Yeah, right!" because it seems impossible
to do. Remember, though, that a major part of trauma recovery
is increasing your self-control, your mastery over your trauma.
That includes taking control of the intrusions of memory that
may be plaguing you or provoking obsessive thoughts. Many of
the keys in this book will help you feel more in control. In addition, there are some tricks you can try also.

Often when trauma survivors are overly preoccupied with
trauma, they need activities to occupy their time and their
mind. You may notice that it is in the spaces where you have
nothing structured that you are most vulnerable. Activities that
people use to fill this kind of space include singing, computer
games, puzzles, beading, car repair, baking, volunteer work,
learning a musical instrument, drawing, or painting. Anything
that occupies both your hands and your mind can be great for
this purpose. During a particularly difficult time, I bought a
book on solitaire games and learned to play about 20 different
ones. It was like an oasis for me. I would get so absorbed in the
games that I would be surprised to discover time had actually
passed without my thinking about my trauma (at first minutes,
then later hours). Once I realized it was possible to create spaces without trauma thoughts, I was able to expand on that idea,
finding other things to do—some more constructive—to pre-
occupy my thoughts.

Some People Become Decidedly Worse From Attention to Their Past.

It is not uncommon for coping mechanisms to weaken or even
fail as individuals focus on past trauma. As mentioned before,
any focus on trauma memories is destabilizing. Some people
can better afford that risk than others. That is, the greater one's

stability prior to dipping into the past, the better one will likely manage. However, when already unstable, or when memory focus causes extreme instability, the cost of spending time in memory may outweigh the benefit. In the next section, I suggest a model you can use to predict if you fall into this category.

Apply a Little Theory

For some of you, the idea that you may not benefit from revisiting your past may come as a hard blow. I know that there are many who become convinced that finding out what happened in the past is the one and only way to a better life. As I said before, for some of you that will be true. For others, though, it will be the opposite—poking around the past could make your life worse. Hopefully the following paragraphs will help you identify which category you might fall into:

- Trauma resolved
- Single trauma
- Multiple trauma, stable
- Multiple trauma, unstable

Trauma Resolved

If you have suffered trauma in your past but it does not intrude on or affect your daily life, you might consider leaving your memories alone. You have probably heard the phrase, "If it ain't broke, don't fix it." It is apt for this situation. Sometimes a well-meaning friend or helping professional will assume that past trauma always means issues to resolve, but that is not the case. Probing the past is only of value when there is something to be gained for the present or future. And, difficult as it is to believe for many, trauma can and does sometimes resolve on its own. So you may be one of the lucky ones who has managed to recover without obvious intervention. Move on and enjoy your life.

Single Trauma

Have you experienced a single trauma that continues to affect you? That might be one incidence of assault, a lone car accident, a molestation, and so on. If there are no other traumas in your history and assuming you are or become stable first (Phase I), processing memory of that trauma could be of use for you. However, that is only if you want to and see a benefit to be gained. Stuart and Stephanie (Key 3) fall into this category.

Multiple Trauma, Stable

For those of you with multiple traumatic events in your past, there are two likely possibilities. The first one involves people who remain resilient despite their experiences. When they reflect on their past, their thought processes are organized and they can address one issue at a time without confusion or intrusion of the other issues. You will know if this is your situation when you can tell someone, or think about, one of your traumas while your attention stays only on that one. If this applies to you, you may also benefit from processing past events once you are stable and safe—if you want to. Liam, in the next chapter, is an example of someone in this category.

Multiple Trauma, Unstable

If you have multiple traumas in your background and they are in a jumble, and thinking or talking about one causes you to be flooded by memories of other events, you might *not* do so well attending to memories. In this situation, attempting to process and resolve a single memory is impossible. The confusion and overwhelming stress that usually ensue in such cases leave the individual in worse condition. Those who continue to attempt processing, hoping they will get through it, often end up in truly difficult circumstances. Stability is what is lacking in these situations, so Phase I work must be the focus. See below for a further discussion of this category with regard to Janice, who you met in the first chapter. For a portion of individuals of this type, successful stabilization may actually result in a change in their status, shifting them into the *multiple trauma, stable* group. When that happens, the other criteria will then apply.

Discovering the Key: Janice, Part 2

Janice is an example of the *multiple trauma, unstable* survivor mentioned above. Her father's incest went on for many years, countless episodes. In addition, her history included being beaten up and bullied at school, as well as three auto accidents.

At the start of our work together, Janice was chaotic. She was often late or forgot sessions altogether. Whenever she delved into her past, she would become completely overwhelmed, often followed by dissociation. The work we did together on managing touch, illustrated in Key 1, was a part of Phase I stabilization. Janice also worked to further control her body and symptoms. She began a program of strength training and took an assertiveness training class. Janice was able to translate what she learned in our relationship to better her relationships with her friends and family. Within 15 months, Janice had developed a network of reliable friends, she was consistent at her job, and she was able to use many tools to control her other symptoms. As a result, her thinking and memory process also stabilized. She was eventually able to focus on one incident at a time without being overwhelmed. At that point she became a better candidate for memory work (Phase II), though she did not choose it. Most people with this kind of overwhelming, multiple trauma history can achieve Janice's level of stability *when the focus is on stability* and then choose if they want to seek out the past. But many are, like Janice, pleased with the changes in their daily life and have little interest in looking backward.

Applications for You

At this point you might be wondering why, when stable enough, anyone would decide to remember past trauma and process his or her recollections. It is not usually pleasant to do, so what could motivate a person to remember something so awful? It is not a particularly good reason to take on such a challenge just because it is there. The only reason to risk the pain and upset involved is if there is something useful to be gained. The importance may lie in clarifying what actually happened or recognizing the meaning of the events. It may have more to do with identifying what went wrong with the hope of preventing anything similar happening to oneself or loved ones in the future. Additional possible benefits, depending on the methodology, include:

- Changing the way you think about yourself as a result of your experience
- Identifying and changing the negative thoughts that keep you bound to the trauma
- Imagining alternative responses that could be useful in the future
- Actually rehearsing defensive impulses or movements that were prevented or frozen during the events such as running away or fighting impulses (e.g., kicking)
- Being able to manage self-defense training
- Reclaiming resources that seem lost to the trauma
- Imagining support that could have prevented the trauma or aided in dealing with the immediate aftermath
- Imagining a different ending

The following exercises will help you decide if it is a good idea for you to spend time on your trauma memories. Do not forget that this is your choice; this chapter and these exercises are for guidance. For those who already know—for whatever reason—that you will or will not be processing trauma memories, these exercises will be unnecessary. If, however, you are in doubt or unsure, they may help you to figure out what is best for you. Before attempting the exercises, remember to check each with your mindful gauge that you developed from the first key. You may discover you would rather skip over one or more of them. Until you have decided one way or the other, stick with stabilizing tasks, many examples of which are outlined in future keys.

Exercise 1: Evaluate Your Stability (Phase I)

1. Are your basic necessities adequately fulfilled? These include safe shelter, food, income, and so on.
2. Are you taking care of yourself: eating regularly, bathing, getting rest, engaging with others?
3. How is your level of general functioning? Are you able to get up in the morning and complete necessary tasks: going to work, cleaning house, making and eating regular meals, laundry?
4. When you become upset, are you able to comfort yourself or reach someone who can help you to calm down?

Exercise 2: Finding Tools to Increase Stability

List specifics of what you need to stabilize and have a better life. Emphasize things you can do in the here and now such as get more exercise, make a new friend, structure your day, and so on. Would it help you to have more activities such as volunteer work or taking an art class? Also consider what you are doing inside yourself. Do you need better control over your thought processes? Maybe you need more knowledge about or skills in dealing with upset or arousal in your nervous system. There could also be very practical things that would improve your stability and quality of life. You might be one who would benefit from a pet, or joining a religious or spiritual group, or perhaps a sports team or book club would be useful for you. The point here is to consider all options. Do not be limited by my examples or the opinions of others. And be alert for anything you might want but do not think possible. It just might be worth looking into as you or someone else might find a way you did not realize was there before.

Exercise 3: Chart Pros and Cons for Revisiting Your Memories

Take a fresh sheet of paper and draw a line down the middle. At the top, label one column "Pro" and one "Con." List your thoughts or arguments for processing trauma memories in the "Pro" column and those against in the "Con" column. You may want to do this all at once or over the course of a few days or weeks and then review your points again. You might also make your lists and then put the paper away for a while. If possible, it could be beneficial for you to talk over these points with a supportive friend, family member, or professional. Be sure it is someone who will respect your decision but will also give you honest feedback on anything you might be missing or overlooking.

Exercise 4: Identify Your Type

Based on the information in the theory section above, assess which trauma type applies to you (trauma resolved; single trauma; multiple trauma, stable; multiple trauma, unstable). Be as honest as you can with yourself, particularly when evaluating your stability and if you can stay focused on one issue at a time. It is important that you acknowledge your limitations, particularly if, when you think about one trauma, others come crashing in and you become easily overwhelmed or debilitated.

Evaluate This Key

Use your mindful gauge and common sense to appraise the value of this key for you. Is making a decision about focusing on the past or present useful for you? Will it be a good idea for you to spend more time on this material or exercises? Imagine scenarios and pay attention to the answer of your gauge. Do not be worried if your gauge tells you that this—or any chapter in this or any other book—is not for you. Finding out what is right for you includes identifying what is not.

Plan How to (or Not to) Use This Key

How will you put to use what you have learned in this chapter? Have you made a decision about your trauma memories? If so, is it a firm decision for always or will you want to revisit your decision in the near or distant future?

Endnote

For those without actual memories, but who have a suspicion of past trauma, some of the most definitive research we have in the trauma field indicates that *false memories* are relatively simple to create. Trying to unearth memory of trauma to account for daily life difficulties is one of the easiest and surest ways to false memory creation. On the other hand, we have many examples of trauma survivors who have or had periods of amnesia for past events, particularly ones of terror or horror. However, attempting to unearth memories for which there is no evidence usually causes more havoc than healing. If you *feel* as though you have been traumatized, but have no memory or information to account for your impressions, stick like glue to the here and now. Emphasize taking control of and easing your symptoms to better your daily life. Avoid delving into an uncertain or unknown past. For too many, that direction has led to severe consequences.

KEY 4

STOP FLASHBACKS

Honesty is the first chapter in the book of wisdom. —THOMAS JEFFERSON

Take care with what you say to yourself, as it actually affects you, particularly when it is about trauma. It has been known for a long time that how we talk to ourselves, what we say inside our heads, makes a huge difference in how we feel emotionally and physically. A great body of research literature confirms this, and the cognitive therapies (e.g., cognitive-behavioral therapy, dialectical behavior therapy, rational emotive therapy, eye movement desensitization and reprocessing) are built upon this foundation. In addition, it is also a matter of common sense and something you can easily demonstrate to yourself (and probably already have). You can test the idea right now by first telling yourself something supportive and then something critical. How does each affect you? Does critical self-talk make you anxious or drag you down? Do comforting words or praise calm you or lift you up?

When it comes to recovering from trauma, your inner dialogue can play a major role in determining how stable or overwhelmed you feel from moment to moment and on a daily basis. To a large degree, your inner dialogue will guide you to recognize the reality of your situation, including your survival, as discussed in Key 2. This key will help you to master your inner dialogue to smooth out and support your recovery from trauma by helping you to change how you talk with yourself about your present reality, particularly flashbacks.

The Issue

Trauma flashbacks, the major feature of PTSD, are not only highly upsetting, they are also extremely confusing. When you are in the throes of a flashback—as the name implies—it can feel as if you are actually being drawn back in the traumatic situation, like it is happening still or again. Flashbacks are intrusive. They strike uninvited, stirring up the images, sensations, and emotions of the original events. A flashback can be so powerful, so overwhelming to one's sense of reality, that many who suffer them believe they are reliving or reexperiencing their trauma. A flashback is able to mimic the real thing because it provokes a similar level of stress in your body. The same hormones course through your veins as did at the time of your actual trauma, setting your heart pounding and preparing your muscles and other body systems to react as they did at that time. You might even move in similar ways, for instance, taking a defensive stance or cowering. For example, many traumatized combat soldiers dive for cover when having a flashback of war experiences. During a flashback, you may see pictures or hear sounds in your mind that enhance the sense of immediacy. And it is usual to describe or talk about a flashback as if it is something that is occurring in the present:

- "It's happening again."
- "I just heard the bomb go off!"
- "He [the attacker] is here in the room."
- "Why does this keep happening again and again?"

For flashbacks to be dampened—or even eliminated—they must be accurately categorized. In reality, a flashback is not a repetition or replay of a past event; it is a *memory* of that event.

This is a critically important distinction and worth repeating: A flashback is a memory. That is the case no matter how intense it is or whether it can fool your mind into believing the trauma is really happening again or still going on.

Notice how the four statements above, the ones concerning incidents from the past, are expressed with present tense verbs. Although this is a typical way for a survivor of trauma to talk during a flashback, those words—expressing past trauma as if it were taking place now—actually make the problem worse. Remember, what you say to yourself matters. If you talk to yourself during a flashback using verbs that indicate it is happening now, it will feel more like now. When describing the past as if it were the present, the same nervous system reactions are evoked that occurred at the time of the actual event. You reel with a comparable degree of terror and confusion. Such upsetting reactions can persist and impact your ability to function in your daily life. Is this happening to you?

A flashback does not need to seize you in that way. Often just a minor editing of terms or verb tense will have a huge impact. Below I discuss two ways language can change your flashback experience. I recommend using both. The first involves simply changing the verbs from present to past tense to describe the flashback. Altering the verb tense will make your dialogue accurate. Notice the difference in these examples:

- "I hear the bomb exploding!" and "When the bomb went off back then, I *heard* it."
- "He's grabbing me!" and "I *was* attacked."

The past tense verbs in the alternative phrases identify that the trauma occurred in the past, that it is part of history. Of course the flashback itself is happening now, so it is true to say "I am having a flashback."

The second way language can be used to alleviate or stop a flashback is to understand it for what it actually is: a memory. A flashback is a very intense recollection of something that has already occurred at an earlier time. Obviously, a flashback is not a typical memory. It is unusual because of its sensory intensity. It can fool you into confusing then with now. Nonetheless, it *is* a memory. I have seen this simple recognition of a flashback as memory have the power to instantly reduce the intensity of, and even stop, a flashback in its tracks.

In reviewing the manuscript for this book prior to publication, my editor, Deborah Malmud, asked a particularly relevant question. She wanted to know why the word flashback was not adequate to indicate the separation of past and present. In her literary mind, the term clearly implied something in the past, flash*back*. However, in truth, I have yet to meet an individual suffering flashbacks who does not experience this confusion at least sometimes. This is why I am such a stickler for the liberal use of the term *memory* in its stead.

Liam, His Past in the Present

Raped by a priest when he was 8, at 32 Liam continued to live as if it was happening again and again. He had frequent and detailed flashbacks of the rape, the rectory where the rape occurred, the priest, and so forth. That single, devastating incident had followed him through his teens, college, and even into his marriage. His wife was very understanding and did her best to bend to Liam's constant need for reassurance and control. However, Liam was losing his tenuous stability and his flashbacks grew more frequent as their son, 7 and a half, approached the age Liam was at the time of his tragedy. Liam and his wife feared how he would manage the boy's eighth year.

Liam often mentioned the rape. I was interested in his language, as he usually used present tense verbs in those references: is, am. I waited until our second meeting before pointing this out to make sure we had established some degree of contact first. I wanted to make sure that he would perceive such feedback as supportive, not critical. When I did finally say, "Have you ever noticed that you tend to speak of the rape with present tense verbs?" he was rather startled. After recovering himself somewhat, he replied, "I guess that is because it feels like it is happening now." Which is, of course, a perfect description of what a flashback is like.

Apply a Little Theory

There are two theoretical bits that are particularly relevant to this key. The first involves enabling the hippocampus to remember trauma in the same way as other life events. The second is concerned with the role of the sensory nervous system in our identification of both our internal and external realities.

The Suppressed Hippocampus

In Key 2, I discussed the critical roles of the hippocampus and amygdala in trauma processing and trauma memory. To remind you, it is typical during trauma for the hippocampus to become overwhelmed by stress hormones, so much so that it may stop functioning well or at all. When that happens, it is not able to give the memory of trauma the accurate time context that helps it to get properly logged into one's past. Without the hippocampal time stamps of beginning, middle, and—especially—*end*, the brain and body will continue to perceive the trauma as ongoing or repeating. This is really the crux of PTSD: the mind and body continuing to respond as though the event persists or recurs on a regular basis.

In Liam's case, and typical of those continuing to suffer from trauma, this meant that he continued to feel and act as if he was being traumatized again and again. The pattern seemed to go on unendingly. To interrupt the sequence, his hippocampus would have to be helped to function properly again. As I said before, many of the keys in this book will assist that. This key, however, is aimed directly toward that goal, to better in-form both mind and body and to help the individual to separate past from present.

In reality, speaking of a past event as if it is happening now is not really honest. Of course a flashback feels like it is happening now, but in truth, it is not. Correcting this only takes a simple adjustment of language, one that accurately expresses fact: the trauma is in the past. Changing verbs to past tense or calling a flashback a memory will accomplish the task. I have seen such a seemingly minor alteration kick-start a trauma survivor—often for the first time—to recognize that the trauma is no longer happening.

Internal and External Reality

Another tool for mediating flashbacks is based in understanding the body's sensory system. Trauma can disrupt the natural regulation of our sensory perception, fooling us that there is danger when there is not and vice versa. Normalizing sensory observation and interpretation can restore a healthy balance, helping the trauma survivor to better judge the reality of situations and surroundings. This will help you, for example, to recognize that the intense sensory aspects of a flashback are being generated in your mind and body, not really in the actual place you are while you are having the flashback.

A little physiology will help to clarify: We have two sensory systems. One of them connects us to our internal reality, the inside of our bodies. The other connects us to our external reality, the world around us. Our external senses are what we usually think of as *the five senses*: hearing, sight, taste, touch, smell. Those senses all gather information from the environment that is external to our bodies (e.g., what you see, hear). The internal senses include balance, the ability to feel what is occurring on the inside (e.g., butterflies in the stomach, pulse, breathing, tremors, muscle aches), and *proprioception*, the facility for locating every part of the body in space (which makes possible, for example, being able to walk safely without looking at your feet).

Usually we use our external senses to evaluate our environment ("Is this situation safe?") and our internal senses to evaluate what is happening inside ("Am I hungry or thirsty?" "Am I sad or happy?"). Unfortunately, though, many people who suffer flashbacks, PTSD, or episodes of anxiety and panic tend to do something quite different. They routinely evaluate their external reality based on what they feel inside, which is backward as well as hazardous. That means, for example, deciding a situation is dangerous based on a feeling of anxiety rather than the evidence of what can actually be seen and heard, or that a street is unsafe to walk down because something there triggers a flashback.

Now, I am not talking about using the mindfulness gauge taught in Key 1 here. That involves using subjective cues from internal states to identify your preferences. And as discussed in that chapter, hopefully you will temper your conclusions with common sense. For mediating a flashback, an *objective* evaluation of your immediate environment and the concrete indicators of physical safety and danger is necessary. Looking around where you are, listening to what is actually happening, and so on is the only way that you (or anyone) will know that your trauma is not happening or that the situation you are in is safe for you or not.

When someone is overwhelmed by a flashback into believing they are reliving or reexperiencing trauma, they are consciously or unconsciously disregarding their actual environment. (The only possible exception would be if they are, for example, really being attacked again. But that would be an additional trauma, not a flashback.) Evaluating external reality by inner sensations is actually how a flashback takes hold. All of the frightening sensory stimuli are generated on the inside of the body, from the memory of the trauma. Something in the environment can certainly trigger the flashback. But triggers are often benign, such as a color or sound. It is as though the traumatized nervous system is always shouting, "Danger, Danger!" The individual may be in the safest place ever but unable to recognize it because of paying more attention to what is going on inside than outside. Likewise, an actual danger may not be noticed because the focus is inward rather than outward.

This is a huge disadvantage. When one cannot perceive true safety, one also cannot perceive actual danger. The situation is similar to the boy who cried wolf. When there finally was real danger, no one was interested in believing him. Lone Reimert (one of two individuals this book is dedicated to) once told me (literally translated), "Recovering from trauma has to do with getting better at being afraid." She meant that a major part of healing from trauma involves regaining the ability to access fear as the protective friend it is meant to be.

To be genuinely safe, you need to see and talk with yourself about situations as they are using *both* internal and external senses. This is the only way you can evaluate an entire situation. For interceding during a flashback there are three vital steps:

1. Attention to the internal experience that is linked to terrifying memory (internal senses).
2. Honest evaluation of the current environment (external senses). In Key 2 Stephanie confirmed this: "We are in a city park and I am 42. I could not be here with you now if I had not gotten away from the wasps back then."
3. Based on the second step, declaring whether or not the present situation is safe.

To accomplish this, you must be willing to consider the possibility that you can feel very afraid *at the same time* that you are in a situation that bears no danger. When you have developed this skill, you will be able to identify when you are in a safe situation even though you may be feeling afraid or having a flashback.

Likewise, you will be better able to identify danger because you will be using your external senses to accurately evaluate your surroundings.

Discovering the Key

The next time Liam went into flashback with me, speaking of the rape as if it was happening now, I intervened.

"Stop, Liam," I said firmly. "It is not happening now. What you are perceiving right now, in my office, is a memory of what happened when you were 8 years old. You are *remembering* when you were raped many years ago. You are now a man. I can see you clearly and am confident that you are not being raped right now."

It took several repetitions to get his attention. Eventually Liam repeated the words, "I am remembering." He said it again, several times. The first few repetitions sounded more like a question than a statement. But by small increments, his agitation decreased. After a few minutes he took a deep breath and looked me in the eye. "That's a memory?" he asked. "Is that what I've been suffering from all this time, a memory?"

"Seems simple on the surface, doesn't it? Of course it is more complex. You certainly suffered the rape at that time. And since, there have been plenty of consequences to deal with: sensations in your body, shame, self-esteem, trust of others, and such. But, yes, the flashbacks you have been plagued by are memories—albeit vivid ones—memories nonetheless."

Liam sighed and placed his head in his hands. He sobbed for a few minutes. When he recovered his composure, he told me that he was deeply sad that he had been raped, and for all the time he had suffered since. It was the first time he had been able to grieve.

Helping Liam to use his external senses at the same time that he was having a flashback was the next step. That took a bit of practice, but eventually he could maintain awareness of his surroundings while having a flashback. Below, in Exercise 2, are instructions for learning to do that yourself.

Liam continued to have periodic flashbacks as we worked for him to gain stability and improve his daily life. As is typical, the flashbacks gradually lost intensity as he became more confident that his present time was free from rape. All told, we spent nearly a year working at this and increasing his stability (Phase I). Once we agreed he was consistently steady, he chose to move on to directly face his memories of the rape (Phase II). For a brief time his flashbacks again increased during that process. But with the foundation of our prior work, he never forgot that he was dealing with memory, pure if not simple.

Applications for You

The recognition that a flashback is indeed a memory may or may not come easily for you. However, once you grasp this truth, it will change your relationship to your traumatic past. Do not become discouraged if this takes you a while. If you keep your eye on the goal, you will likely be pleased with the result.

The exercises below are designed to develop your skill. Eventually, they will help you to recognize a flashback for the memory that it really is, something that happened in your past. As you try them, have in mind that the aim is to help your trauma memories to rest in the past where they belong, to stop them from intruding on your daily life, your now.

There is one main criterion for deciding if the exercises that follow will be appropriate for you: Do you have flashbacks? If the answer is no, then these exercises are not for you, though some of the principles may be useful for other situations. However, if you do have flashbacks, first consider if there would be any negative consequences if you gain control over them. Most of you will be relieved to gain mastery of your flashbacks, but I have encountered a couple of individuals for whom that idea was somewhat threatening. If that applies to you, put off these exercises until you feel more comfortable with the concepts of this chapter and the goals of the exercises.

Exercise 1: A Second Mantra

It may seem too simplistic, but try this anyway. Just be accurate: Your flashback is a memory, not a repeat of your trauma. Next time you have a flashback, remind yourself in clear words (in your head, out loud, from a voice recorder, or on a piece of paper you can pull out and read) that it is a memory, that the trauma is not happening now. If you cannot do it yet during the flashback, then make sure to once the flashback abates. "That was a memory. As real as it may have felt, it was not happening now." Write down a few different ways to express this idea and choose one or two that make the most sense to you or try them out and see what works best. You might carry a card in your pocket with those words, so you can pull it out when you need it. Some people put the message on a voice mail to themselves or on their cell phone's voice recorder.

Exercise 2: Mantra Specific

Liam embellished the basic idea and created a new mantra for himself. When he would have a flashback he would say, "I am remembering what happened to me when I was 8. That was 24 years ago. It hasn't happened since and it's not happening now. It was awful and it is awful to remember. *And* I am glad it is a memory and no longer really happening."

How would you most accurately express the truth of your own present situation? Jot down a few different formulations using Liam's as inspiration. Try it out and edit. Keep revising until you find the words that are just right for you. Also note, it is crucial that you do not include any details of your trauma in this mantra. Adding details could risk intensifying a flashback rather than dampening it. Make sure to keep your sentences succinct.

Exercise 3: Flashback Protocol

You can apply this structured procedure several ways (adapted from my first book, *The Body Remembers*):

- During a flashback to stop or reduce its impact
- As a preparation for a situation you are facing that you anticipate could trigger a flashback
- As a morning ritual, so that it becomes automatic whenever you need it (the way a fire drill in school prepares kids to react safely in the event of a real fire)

You can also teach this to a friend or family member so that they can coach you during a flashback. Some people record the sequence on their mobile phone or other recording device to be available at the push of a button.

The steps are outlined below. However, please use your own common sense and your mindful gauge to help you edit the protocol into something that suits you. Try it different ways and see what works best for you.

If you become more distressed when sensing your body, skip the first step and start with the second. You may be able to add that in later when you are feeling more secure, but it is not necessary for the protocol to be successful.

1. Pay attention to your internal senses, naming one or more sensations you have, such as heart rate, changes in respiration, dizziness, sweaty palms, shaky legs, cold hands, or butterflies in your stomach.
2. Identify what you are feeling emotionally, for example, "I am afraid."
3. State clearly to yourself that these symptoms are in re-

action to a *memory*. You may give the flashback a title if you want, but make sure the title is no more than three words: "I am having these symptoms because I am remembering The Assault."

4. Shift attention to your external senses and name at least three things you can see, hear, or smell: "I can hear the lawn mower next door." "I see the sun shining through the front window." "I smell cinnamon from the bread in the toaster."

5. Affirm today's date, including the year, month, and day.

6. Based on the information from the last two steps, evaluate if the situation you are in now is safe or dangerous.

7. If you are actually safe, in spite of having a flashback, you can then tell yourself, "I am having a flashback *and* I am not in any danger." Or "[the title of the trauma] is not happening now (or anymore)."

8. If you are not in safe circumstances, seek safety.

Here is an example of the protocol put all together. Remember, your statement may be quite different. Just be sure to include the pertinent elements.

"I am really scared and my heart is racing and I am shivering cold, because I am remembering the attack when I was 10. At the same time I am looking around my living room and I can see my green couch, my flat-screen television, and my husband's shoes. I can also hear the microwave beeping that the leftovers are warm and I can hear my son yelling at his sister. By the calendar I can see it is 30 years later. So I know that the attack was a long time ago and not happening now (or again)."

Evaluate This Key

Use your mindful gauge and common sense to evaluate if identifying your flashbacks as memories is helpful to you. Though I am quite confident in the usefulness of the flashback protocol, I also know that nothing works for everyone. If it has potential for you but does not work, try various edits until you find the form that suits you best. If it does not work for you, set it aside. You might revisit it later, or eliminate it from your repertoire.

Plan How to (or Not to) Use This Key

Where and when would it be best for you to be reminded that your memories are of the past and that your flashbacks are memories? Are you best off waiting until a flashback occurs, or will you benefit most from planning and rehearsing for future flashbacks?

How will you remind yourself? A note on the bathroom mirror? Writing or drawing on your hand? Some people purchase or designate an object (coin, stone, iPod, cell phone) they can have with them as an anchor to the present. When having a flashback of childhood trauma, for instance, you can pull your mobile phone from your pocket or purse to remind you it is now the present day. Experiment to find what would work best for you.

RECONCILE FORGIVENESS AND SHAME

Self-forgiveness is essential to self-healing.   —RUTH CARTER STAPLETON

Part A. Forgive Your Limitations

For some of you, the key to trauma recovery will be most concerned with reconciling feelings of guilt or shame that have lingered following your trauma. In general, particularly with trauma, shame and forgiveness are often linked. For that reason, I will address them as aspects of this same key: "Forgive Your Limitations" is Key 5A, and "Share Your Shame" is Key 5B.

Most of the self-help books that address forgiveness focus on forgiving others. In this chapter, however, I would like to pay attention to a somewhat neglected aspect of forgiveness that is particularly relevant for trauma survivors: self-forgiveness. Is it difficult for you to forgive yourself for your trauma? If so, you are not alone.

You may remember the January 2009 plane crash that came to be known as "the Miracle on the Hudson." Pilot Chesley "Sully" Sullenberger managed to safely water ditch an Airbus 320 only minutes into the flight; it had lost both engines due to a bird strike during takeoff. Every one of the 155 passengers and crew survived, with only 2 seriously injured—truly a miracle. In his first television interview following this incident that made him a famous hero, Captain Sullenberger confessed to *60 Minutes'* Katie Couric, "One of the hardest things for me to do in this whole experience was to forgive myself for not having done something else, something better, something more complete."

Sullenberger's candor actually stunned me. His admission underscored how self-forgiveness is a critical and universal issue in trauma recovery. If anyone ever qualified to skip the forgiveness issue, this man—who saved every single life on his crippled airplane and, moreover, has the undying gratitude of hundreds of passengers' loved ones, plus the admiration of his colleagues and perhaps most of the world—should be at the top of the list. All the same, self-forgiveness was something he, too, struggled with.

As with Captain Sully, forgiving yourself could be difficult and deserves to be high on your recovery to-do list. Given that you live with and depend on yourself 24/7, having a peaceful inner relationship can make your life and recovery easier. No matter how rationally you may see your culpability, being angry or disappointed with yourself for not being able to prevent or stop trauma is common. There may be legitimate cause for your self-anger. It may be that you actually could have done one or more things that would have kept you or another out of harm's way. It could also be the case that there was nothing you could have done, that the full responsibility lies with someone else or chance. In most cases, though, the truth is somewhere in between. Here are a few examples:

1. Sandra had a car accident. She was not at fault. The other driver ran a red light. However, Sandra also knew that she had been in a hurry. When her traffic light turned green, she was the first into the intersection. Had she been slightly less rushed, she might have seen that the offending car had no intention of stopping for his red light. Legally, the responsibility went to the other driver. But Sandra also had to recognize and then forgive herself for not taking an extra few seconds to ensure all of the cross-traffic had stopped.

2. When Peter was 9, he was badly beaten by a couple of older boys who caught him on his way home from school. There was no way he could have foreseen the attack as he did not know the boys and he had never been threatened on the route to or from school before. It was really an attack out of nowhere. Moreover, he was outweighed and outnumbered. Nonetheless, he still felt responsible and needed help to let himself off the hook.

3. A woman I called "R" in one of my early articles was raped while on vacation in a foreign country. She had accepted the invitation of a local young man to show her the sights of his city, leaving the company of her traveling companions to go off with him alone. After looking around the city, she agreed to go with him to ruins that were outside the city. It was there that he, along with one of his friends, entrapped her. There were many aspects to helping R recover from the rape, self-forgiveness being one. We carefully distinguished her responsibility from that of the rapist. Without a doubt, the young man was responsible for the nasty setup and the rape itself. He had planned to rape her from his first invitation, arranging for his friend to meet them at the ruins. At the same time, R made two risky decisions: leaving her group of friends and later traveling with the man out of the city. She needed to reconcile both of those misjudgments.

Allocating responsibility can be a delicate matter. Some people take on much that is not theirs; others abdicate any and all. However, striking an honest balance is important. For one thing, it is sane-making. Second, it can help you to better protect yourself, and perhaps your loved ones, in the future. For R, realizing how she could have been a more savvy foreign visitor helped her to advise her daughters when they were old enough to travel with friends.

Understandably, forgiveness is a large topic involving people, circumstances, and for some, the spiritual realm. It is not possible to address all of these facets within the confines of this chapter. Through the pages that follow, the discussion will cover the most universal aspect of trauma-related forgiveness, self-forgiveness for:

- Not being able to foresee, prevent, or stop the trauma from happening
- Running away instead of fighting back
- Going "dead," not being able to flee or fight

This chapter will help you to identify what was and what was not your responsibility and in your control. The next chapter, Key 5B, will help you to understand, accept, and resolve any shame that has resulted from trauma, which often goes hand in hand with self-forgiveness. Which one you tackle first will be up to your unique circumstances. It may be necessary to forgive yourself before you can resolve your shame. Alternatively, it could be your shame that needs to be addressed prior to self-forgiveness. You might use your mindful gauge to decide which to prioritize.

Please note: It will likely be the fewest readers of this book who have actually caused trauma, either by direct intent (e.g., perpetrating on another) or through disregard for the safety of others (e.g., causing injury to others while behaving recklessly or under the influence of drugs or alcohol). If you fall into this category, facing up to regret and reparation will be necessary prerequisites to self-forgiveness.

The Issue

One fact of trauma is that it is out of your control. *Everyone* who has suffered trauma has issues about control because trauma does not happen when you have it—when you can stop the car, fend off the attacker, defuse the bomb, and so on. If you are recovering from trauma, you also were unable to stop whatever it was that happened. There may be one reason you could not prevent your trauma or there might be several. Here are some (but not all) possibilities:

- You were not old, big, or strong enough, or you were outnumbered.
- You did not have the help you needed.
- Someone made a mistake.
- It was an unpreventable act of nature.
- There was no alert or warning.
- You did not have the legal rights necessary.
- You were in the wrong place at the wrong time.
- You were lied to, threatened, or coerced.
- You did not have adequate or correct information or training.
- You froze, dissociated, or "went dead."

This is not a complete list. The reason you were unable to prevent your trauma may not be here. Feel free to add to this list.

Helen is a good example of someone who should be able to justify many reasons why her trauma was not her fault. Nonetheless, she really suffered under the weight of guilt for being caught in the Indian Ocean tsunami in December 2004. She had arranged the vacation that eventually put her family at risk. Luckily, they all survived. Even so, she felt culpable for bringing her family there and for their distress. It had been particularly difficult for her youngest daughter, who still had nightmares a year later. Helen, as well as thousands of others who were caught in that disaster, met the criteria for several of the categories above: unpreventable act of nature, no warning, wrong place at the wrong time, and not getting enough help.

Understanding that what had happened was not Helen's fault was clear for her friends, and even her family; however, she had a very tough time letting herself off the hook. It was actually her teenage son who finally tipped the balance for her. One evening he became very irritated with her persistent guilty apologies and barked at her, "Stop it, Mom! Who do you think you are, God? Only God knew that was going to happen. IT WAS NOT YOUR FAULT!" Whether it was his words, his timing, or something else, finally the message got through. At first she was angered by his attitude, but then she laughed. As she took in his words, she sat down and cried.

When I next saw her, she was smiling, remembering her son's anger and how much his outburst had helped her. "He's right, you know," she told me. "That was sort of arrogant to think I should be able to predict nature. It really wasn't my fault! I'm sleeping better now, and so is my daughter." It seemed that once Helen could let go of her guilt, her daughter also improved.

The sudden change in Helen might sound like a miracle cure because it seems to have happened in a few short minutes. However, her release from guilt and subsequent self-forgiveness was actually the result of a combination of factors, including her work with a number of recovery strategies (several in this book). Her persistent efforts, the support of her family and friends, and her son's lucky timing all culminated to push her over the hump that had been holding her back. Recovery from trauma takes time, but sometimes, as with Helen, the facets can suddenly gel, making it look like recovery was instantaneous, even though it may actually have been in process gradually over time.

Apply a Little Theory

As if experiencing trauma were not enough, many trauma survivors suffer further with regret for how they did or did not react. They may feel responsible for "going dead," becoming paralyzed, not fighting back or running away. Familiarity with the basic neurobiology of the trauma response often helps understanding of such responses, contributing to relief from self-directed anger, shame, and guilt.

Survival—keeping us alive in our environment—is mediated by the limbic system in the midbrain. The amygdala and hippocampus are both part of the limbic system's survival team, the amygdala being particularly relevant for this discussion. Before reading on, you might want to review the earlier discussions of these structures on pages 30–32.

The amygdala determines what is or is not a threat following its perception of information from the external senses (see Key 4): A touch or something seen, heard, or smelled. That sensory information is first quickly relayed to the amygdala for evaluation: "Is this desirable, benign, or dangerous?" If it is life-threatening, the amygdala can direct the body to respond with any of three options: flight, fight, or freeze.

There is a myriad of information upon which the amygdala bases its decision, including the following:

- What is the physical condition of this body?
- How has it been able to respond to something similar in the past?
- What are we up against?
- Is there a likelihood that flight or fight would be successful?

Remember, all of this happens very quickly and—critical to note—not in the cortex, the seat of thought, reflection, and contemplation in the brain. The amygdala's survival response is set in motion outside our awareness. It is processing data, coming to a conclusion, and directing action totally without conscious deliberation. It makes its decision and tells the body to run, to attack, or to play dead, sending its directive through the nervous system to the muscles and other body systems. The amygdala sends its order via stress hormones, that is, without the benefit (or interference) of the cortical tools of logic, reason, or even common sense. It is the job of the amygdala to bypass thinking so it can make a swift determination of the situation and cause the body to react—almost immediately—in the best interests of survival.

So when faced with a threat, your nervous system is designed to make an extremely quick decision, which is a great advantage. Think about the consequences if that was not possible, if you had to go through the laborious process of consciously deciding what to do or how to respond. You would have to think clearly about what was happening, identify your options for survival, and then weigh the possible outcomes—all before you could react. By the time you came to any kind of conclusion, it is likely that the threat would have gotten to you without a chance for any kind of survival action. It is actually fantastic that we are unable to decide consciously to escape, battle, or collapse. The amygdala's quick action saves many, many lives. However, there may be consequences to contend with.

Josh's Freeze

Forty-year-old Josh grew up in a liberal community. He knew he was gay from the time of his first crush, when he was about 11. It was never an issue for his family or friends. He was loved and supported and had been in a committed relationship for 8 years. On weekends together with friends, he would enjoy the gay scene in a trendy part of the city. Sometimes things would get a little rowdy, but incidents were minor. Then one day, he was taken completely by surprise—as is so typical with trauma—and his life changed.

Josh, his partner, and two of their friends became victims of a hate crime, attacked as they were returning to their car after an evening on the town. They were harassed and beaten by a gang of self-described antigay vigilantes. Luckily, a neighbor by the parking lot heard the clash and called the police. They arrived in time to arrest the attackers and save Josh and his friends from permanent physical harm. But the police were not able to prevent severe emotional damage, particularly to Josh.

Of the four, Josh fared the worst psychologically. He was not a physical kind of guy and had never studied any kind of self-defense system. While his friends were, to some extent, able to fight back, Josh collapsed in a typical freeze reaction. In the days, weeks, and months following the attack, he sank deeper and deeper into depression.

On the surface, it could be easy to assume that Josh's troubles stemmed from some deep identity conflict that was released by the attack. Another assumption might be that he was emotionally hurt by the verbal abuse of the attackers or angry at the injustice. But none of these were at the core of Josh's difficulties. The truth of the matter was that Josh was deeply ashamed. His humiliation was not due to what was done to him, but because he was not able to fight back. He felt that the beatings he and his friends received were his fault, that he should have been able to stop the attackers, to protect his partner and his friends. There is no dispute that the attack was shameful. Hate crimes are just plain wrong. So why was Josh placing the weight of responsibility on himself?

Discovering the Key

Josh had never known about the freeze response. He just assumed he had been a coward. The realization that a part of his unconscious brain had made the decision for him was a huge relief. It was also helpful for him to learn that the limbic system could be updated with new information and body experiences. For example, learning defensive moves or increasing aerobic endurance could improve the chance of the amygdala choosing flight or fight in the future (though it is never a guarantee—even self-defense experts can still freeze if the amygdala perceives that is the best strategy). He resolved to get in better physical shape and take a self-defense class or two. Though he hoped never to be attacked again, he wanted to be able to use his fight reflex should he ever need it in the future. His new knowledge and resolve helped relieve his depression. But he still had to face himself and forgive the reaction he did have.

The technique that proved most useful for Josh involved envisioning that the exact same attack had happened to another group of friends. I suggested that Josh imagine one of his best friends in his own circumstances, feeling guilty and ashamed for not fighting back. What would he say to the friend? Would he judge or condemn him as he had himself? Or would he be more likely to support him? What would he say to his friend?

At first Josh thought that the exercise was a bit absurd. Of course he would never criticize or malign a friend who had been attacked like that. The real challenge came when I asked why on earth, if he would not criticize a friend like that, he would criticize himself. That brought him up short to realize how much harder he was on himself than he ever would be on anyone else. Josh prided himself on fairness and was distressed to grasp how unfair he was being with himself. That realization greatly facilitated his self-forgiveness, making it possible for him to get back to his normal life.

Applications for You

Many of you will be able to identify with Josh's dilemma, as you will also have gone into a freeze response (dissociation, collapse, numbing, paralysis, deadness) during the incident that threatened your life or limb. Sometimes it is difficult for people to understand that this is really a survival response because they see it as giving up. However, freezing has many functions that protect you.

First of all, when you freeze, your attacker may lose interest. In the animal kingdom, most predators have instincts to avoid dead meat. So when their prey drops, freezing and appearing dead, the predator will often walk away—that is, unless it is very, very hungry and willing to risk bacteria or food poisoning. Among humans, many an attacker will back off if there is no energy coming from the victim. If a victim no longer engages them, many perpetrators will just go away. (Actually, Josh was the least injured of the four as the attackers focused on the three who were defending themselves.) Typically, in a freeze state, time slows down and some people have reported this actually made conscious strategizing possible (though that is not always the case). Finally, people who have survived mauling by an animal tell of a dampening of physical pain and emotional horror in the state of freeze. The dulling of the experience helped them to endure and also suppressed their fear of death. So freezing is a very important and useful reaction. It is good that we are able to freeze. It is not in any way the same as giving up or voluntarily submitting (though there are circumstances where it could be wise to so). Freezing protects you. When you freeze, the amygdala is doing its job just as it should. But of course sometimes, as in Josh's case, that can be difficult to accept.

Is self-forgiveness of your limitations one of your recovery tasks? If so, are you ready for this step? As with most things in life, timing is important. Pushing you toward that goal prematurely could backfire. The main prerequisite for self-forgiveness of limitations is an openness to the possibility that you may not have had a choice in how you reacted during your trauma. If you can entertain that concept, then the exercises below may prove useful for you. However, if that idea is beyond your comprehension at this time, wait before attempting them. You can return to them at any time.

Exercise 1: Learn the Theory

The task of forgiving trauma response limitations—not being able to escape or fight back—is one that is often helped by a thorough understanding of the neurobiology; it is difficult to argue with science. This is also an issue socially and in the legal system, which compounds the problem for trauma survivors. Society in general and the law in particular have been slow to recognize the legitimacy of the freeze response, particularly that it is not—in any way—the same as consent. Throughout the 1980s and 1990s, trauma specialists and researchers in the United States and other parts of the world worked diligently to educate lawyers and judges to identify freezing as a nonvoluntary physiological consequence of threat (e.g., in assault or rape). At the time of this writing, most legal systems now recognize that when victims have not fought back it in no way implies they were willing. So, if the court system can accept this as fact, hopefully that will help you to also.

Reread the theory section of this chapter, perhaps writing a summary in your own words. As you better understand the freeze mechanism, it will be easier for you to accept and forgive such responses in yourself.

Exercise 2: In Someone Else's Shoes

Similar to what Josh did above, consider how you would feel if your best friend or someone else you love were in your same situation, the one you are having trouble forgiving yourself for. Would you hold him or her responsible? If not, what makes the difference between you? How could you direct your compassion for your friend toward yourself? Create a conversation (in your mind or by writing it down) between you and that friend. What would you say to him or her about guilt and about self-forgiveness? Can you say similar things to yourself?

If you would hold your friend responsible, what would you consider a fair reparation? Would that also be acceptable for you?

Exercise 3: Talk With Others

It could be helpful as well as supportive to talk with one or more trusted friends or family members about their own experiences with self-forgiveness. You could also discuss how they might feel were they in your shoes. Would it be difficult or easy to forgive themselves? Why or why not?

Evaluate this Key

Is self-forgiveness an issue for you? There is no reason to make it an issue, if it is not. Inclusion of this chapter does not mean that everyone will have something to forgive themselves for. You can use your mindful gauge and common sense to help guide you to determine if and when to address self-forgiveness.

Plan How to (or Not to) Use This Key

In general, being kind toward and forgiving of our human limitations is beneficial, though of course it is important to learn from mistakes and admit failings. But I find most people are harder on themselves than they need to be. How can you make the most of this key in your life? If you meditate or say prayers, perhaps you could add something about self-forgiveness to your practice.

Endnote

Though not specifically addressed in this chapter, there are certainly additional consequences of trauma that could impact your relationship to yourself. You may have other or additional reasons to take a look at self-forgiveness. You may be holding yourself responsible or condemning yourself for these things:

- Not being able to save another
- Damage to or loss of property or money
- Surviving when another did not

If so, achieving self-forgiveness in those areas will also help your recovery.

Another area in need of self-forgiveness may be your patience with yourself and the pace of your recovery. If you are not healing "fast enough," anger at yourself will just worsen the situation. Recovery takes the time it takes. Attempting to hurry it often actually slows it down.

We need to realize shame can have great value, as long as we are not over-whelmed by it.   —RONALD & PATRICIA POTTER-EFRON

Everyone needs a sense of shame, but no one needs to feel ashamed.

—NIETZCHE

Part B. Share Your Shame

Shame is a major concern for many survivors of trauma. It is awful to experience. No one likes feeling ashamed. Neverthe-less, believe it or not, shame is just like all of our other emotions and feelings—it is necessary for our survival. This section (5B) goes hand in hand with the previous one (5A) as shame and self-forgiveness are often (but not always) interlinked. At times it is self-forgiveness that must be achieved before shame can be re-lieved; at other times resolution of shame is the prerequisite to self-forgiveness. Together these two sections constitute Key 5.

Quite simply, our shame tells us—deeply—that something is amiss. Without that important knowledge, we would have little opportunity to avoid, change, or repair whatever is wrong. Many who have experienced trauma grapple with feelings of shame connected to it. For some, resolving shame is the most difficult aspect of trauma recovery. In these next pages, I will make a case for the central role shame plays in human evolu-tion and help you to identify the role it played (or plays) in your trauma survival and recovery.

With most things, any kind of extremes are not usually help-ful. Shame is no different in that regard: It is neither good to have too much nor too little shame. You might be surprised that I would consider the absence of shame to be a disadvan-tage. However, a good many of you reading this book have ac-tually suffered the harmful consequences that can result from someone who lacks shame—most violent and sexual offenders are apt examples of just that. In fact, I would argue, *shameless-*

ness is a much worse problem in society as a whole than shame itself.

The Issue

Shame is widespread in the wake of trauma. Often it has to do with an inner feeling of letting oneself down, not being able to protect the self. Such a feeling of shame can result from any type of traumatic incident. More specifically, assault, rape, sexual molestation, and incest are the traumas most prone to a debilitating level of shame in the survivor. A major difficulty in dealing with shame is the withdrawal it evokes. Universally, when feeling shame, the tendency is to withdraw. I am reminded of a dinner with European friends a few years ago. I sat with the family of five, including three children aged 3, 4, and 7. Suddenly the 4-year-old snatched an attractive morsel from the plate of the 3-year-old—who, of course, began to cry. The parents reacted with verbal shock. Though it was a language I did not speak, I could distinctly hear the disapproval in their voices and see it in their faces. The 4-year-old blushed deeply, dropped her head, and proceeded to wrap herself up in the nearby window curtains. It was a while before she emerged again and tentatively finished her meal while evading contact with the rest of us. Luckily her parents were savvy and made the effort to reestablish contact with her after dinner. The incident underscored several aspects of shame for me:

- How immediate and physical the nature of shame is
- Its role in shaping social behavior (I doubt the child ever stole food from another's plate again)
- The importance of contact in resolving shame

You may have noticed in yourself or observed in someone else that it is common when ashamed to duck the head and avoid eye contact. Physical withdrawal such as leaving the room or situation is also quite normal with shame. Though natural, this tendency to seclusion when feeling ashamed is often unfortunate. The consequences of trauma are frequently isolating in themselves. Adding shame to the mix can leave the survivor feeling (and even being) very, very alone.

Two Cases

Eileen

It would be an understatement to call the family Eileen grew up in dysfunctional. Her tyrannical father controlled his wife and four children in every aspect of their lives. He moved them to a remote rural area and demanded that his wife homeschool the children. Frequently he would fly into rages and take out his anger in a physical way. As his favorite, Eileen was spared beatings but singled out for sex throughout her teen years. She was given special privileges including small gifts and a room of her own. In addition, he never hit her. Eileen's feelings of shame festered and multiplied over the years: for not being able to protect herself, her mother, and her siblings; for submitting to incest; for never being beaten.

Eileen had tried many types of therapy. She had been through her history and specific incidents over and over again. Though much of the therapy had been helpful, she continued to be haunted by intense feelings of shame. "I am a terrible person," she told me with bowed head when I first met her.

Remember, shame is like every other emotion; it has a survival function. This is no less true in the case of an incest survivor such as Eileen. Shame is like a beacon, pointing out that what happened was terribly, terribly wrong. One of the difficulties, however, especially with sexual abuse, is that innocent victims almost universally feel like the beacon is shining on them, that it is they who are wrong. I believe that has something to do with the nature of sexual abuse. Molestation, incest, and rape are not perpetrated by people who are feeling shame themselves. An active feeling of shame would stop a potential abuser before he could act—that is a major function of the emotion. Since Eileen's father felt no shame, Eileen—in a sense—ended up feeling it for him. Truly—at least in part—his shamelessness caused her shame.

Max

By the turn of the 21st century, Vietnam veteran Max was—he believed—well adjusted to civilian life. However, he continued to react to reminders of his combat experiences. Notably, witnessing war on television news, documentaries, or films could cause his hands to shake and tears to flow. One recent evening while dining with friends, a passenger jet flew low and loud over the house. All of a sudden, Max found himself under the table. He had taken the posture of a marine diving for cover into a bunker. His friends later told him that he had been "wild-eyed" and "senseless" for about 2 minutes.

Max remembered few details of the episode. Nonetheless, he was left with a deep feeling of shame. "After all of these years, you would think I would know better!" he accused himself. For many months he declined all invitations. He was afraid of the same thing happening again. His shame intruded on his friendships and social life, isolating him as it does so many trauma survivors. Eventually, it drove him to seek help.

Also, in Max's case the shame was telling him that something was wrong. In this case it was his circumstances that were amiss. Max was suffering from PTSD, and though he had been able to put much of it aside (at least temporarily), he had not really gotten the help that he needed to permanently leave his war experiences behind. The town he lived in had few services for traumatized veterans, and his military friends often scoffed at comrades who were candid about their PTSD. Max had, in essence, gone underground with his suffering and was ashamed that he had been exposed at the dinner. It is a widespread dilemma with military trauma that it is just not yet acceptable for soldiers to be emotionally affected by their service. Many military personnel who have PTSD feel shame for what they perceive (and often is regarded) as a weakness. It is my hope that this book and my other publications are making a significant contribution to normalizing this condition.

Apply a Little Theory

There are two main topics for this theory section. The first part concerns shame specifically. The second part focuses on how military and society views on PTSD exacerbate shame in those afflicted.

The Specifics of Shame

It is now fairly well recognized by anthropologists, psychologists, and sociologists that shame has (and has had) a necessary role in the evolution of any culture or society. Among other things, shame shapes socialization, guiding our behavior to make us accepted members of our families, neighborhoods, and cultures. Shame is necessary to help the "tribe" to survive. The shame of incest is a good example. Most people (except the shameless, of course) have a deep-seated feeling of shame even at the thought of—let alone attempt at—incest. This is extremely advantageous. It ultimately prevents rampant inbreeding which, because of damage to the gene pool, could eventually weaken or even extinguish a lineage or cultural group.

Essentially, shame is an indicator that a behavior or state of affairs is just plain wrong. That was certainly the case for both Eileen and Max. His shame was telling him that he was still suffering from the war, something he had been trying to deny for a long time. In Eileen's situation, just about everything was wrong: how she was treated, how her mother and siblings were treated, the violence, the incest, and so on. In both instances, it was the weight of their shame that motivated them to seek help.

Despite its survival value, most would agree that shame remains the most difficult of the emotions to resolve. It is unlike other feelings. When you are sad, you can often find relief in crying. Anger might ease with verbal expression or physical activity. Fear releases in shaking or with comfort and safety. But shame—what do you do with shame? It does not seem to release in the same way other emotions do. Though all feelings are managed better in supportive contact with others, resolution of shame seems to call for it. Rather than discharging (as, for example, crying or yelling), shame *dissipates*, when it is understood or acknowledged by a supportive other. More than any other feeling, I find that shame needs contact to diminish. This makes a certain amount of sense, as shame is a highly social emotion. If humans lived each in isolation, it is not so likely we would feel shame. It requires the presence of others to make its impact. So then it seems reasonable that interaction would be a necessary component for healing shame.

Accepting PTSD

The term *posttraumatic stress disorder* is made up of several concepts, the core of which is *stress*. Simply put, stress is the body's response to any demand, good or bad—it is easy to forget that fun or exciting activities and challenges can also exert stress on the body. There are lesser and greater degrees of stress. The demands of trauma cause the most extreme stress responses.

Traumatic stress results from a threat to life or limb. This includes accidents, war, physical injury, natural disasters, assault, rape, and sexual abuse. It is actually a desirable response, at least initially. It is traumatic stress that makes it possible for your body to flee, fight, or freeze. As discussed in the previous section on forgiveness, the amygdala in the limbic system quickly evaluates a situation and directs the necessary somatic response via stress hormones. These reactions ensure protection or escape when that is possible. When neither of those are options, then it directs the body to freeze, dampening the impact of whatever is to come. Traumatic stress—with its rush of adrenaline—is the protection nature provides to help us survive trauma.

However, the traumatic stress response is intended to be short-lived, lasting just long enough to get us through. Once the incident is over, the body is meant to return to a balanced state. However, sometimes the limbic system's other key structure, the hippocampus (see Key 1), becomes so overwhelmed by stress hormones that it is unable to perceive the cessation of the traumatic incident. When that happens, the amygdala continues to direct the release of stress hormones as if the trauma repeats or persists, causing the same stress reactions to go on and on and on. That is really the crux of PTSD. As discussed in the case of Josh in Key 5A, no one gets to choose how much stress hormone is released during trauma or whether or not their hippocampi (we have two, one on each side of the brain) function well or become suppressed.

Unfortunately, as of this writing, we do not yet have definitive information on the factors that distinguish those who develop PTSD from those who do not, though this is an area of continuing study. Major candidates include attachment styles, previous exposure to trauma, stress preparation, contact, and support.

The point is, *it is not your fault if you have PTSD*. It is not Max's fault. It occurs in about 20–25% of the population who experience trauma. Hopefully the keys in this book as well as other books and therapies you have used or will use will greatly help your recovery. Liberal amounts of self-acceptance, support, and patience are also important ingredients.

Discovering the Keys

For Eileen, there were several steps involved in dealing with the depth of her shame. The first was to understand that the feeling of shame was absolutely sensible: What her father had done was 100% wrong. Considering that her shame had, in part, been confirming the wrong that had been done to her was a new idea to digest. Though at first it was somewhat confusing, the concept gradually made sense to her. The realization helped Eileen move "the beacon" to illuminate what should have been her father's shame, his shameful acts.

Her next task involved specifically distinguishing or separating the shame she felt about herself from the shame of his acts. One of the strategies she used was fairly simple. Dividing a sheet of paper into two columns, she labeled one for herself and one for her father. Under each heading, she listed the shameful acts of each. Her father's list was very long. When it came to her own list, though, she balked. She could only identify things that were directly related to what her father had done to her or others in the family, such as "giving in to his advances" or "not protecting my brother." She was a bit stunned to see, in black and white, that her shame was completely tied to his shameless acts. Increasingly it sank in that she was not the terrible person she had always believed herself to be, but a legitimately innocent victim. That realization made it possible for her to draft a letter to her father clarifying in her own mind and feelings what had been his responsibility and, therefore, his shame. We discussed the advisability of actually sending such a letter. She decided not to, concluding that her father was not going to "see the light" and acknowledge his wrongdoing. Writing the letter had been satisfying in itself. She felt as if she had, in essence, delivered his shame back to him.

The final step Eileen took in resolving her shame was to confide in a trusted friend. After securing the friend's willingness, Eileen *outlined* (but did not detail—no reason to risk trauma to the friend) the extent of her father's abuse and how he had used her. The friend's horror at what he had done was helpful to Eileen in reinforcing her own innocent position. Sharing her shame with that accepting and caring friend added to the healing process considerably. It was a significant stride toward Eileen's eventual relief from the weight of her shame.

For Max, it was the isolation his shame inflicted upon him that was doing the most damage. Getting him to talk with family and friends was helpful. However, sharing his experiences then and now with other soldiers turned out to be the most healing for him. It was not easy for Max to approach the Department of Veterans Affairs (VA) initially. His shame was nearly paralyzing, and was compounded by his assumption that he would be scoffed at and further shamed for his PTSD. With the support of his older brother, he found his way to the social work office at the nearest VA. A caseworker there assured him that he was not alone, that there were many other vets struggling with the same issues.

Through the social work department Max was referred to a support group. He had to drive to the nearest city to meet with a group of Vietnam veterans, but it turned out to be well worth that extra time. Up until then he had avoided other vets for fear that they would judge him a coward. But in the support group he joined, he found quite the contrary. Not only were they very accepting of his difficulties, many of them had suffered similar problems; he was not at all alone in his reactions. Lots of the other guys had had at least one similar experience of plunging for protective cover as if they were under attack from the enemy—triggered by a passing plane, a car backfiring, thunder, an earthquake, and such. Many of them also reacted to news reports and films that highlighted war. When Max realized that all these years his most humiliating, fear-driven, and isolating behaviors were quite common among his comrades, his shame eased considerably. Periodic guest speakers were one of the features of the support group. Max found the lecture on the physiology of PTSD to be particularly helpful in normalizing his condition. He still was not happy to have PTSD, but the shame about it was rapidly dissipating.

Eventually, Max became an activist. Though he acknowledged that the military had come a long way in recognizing PTSD as a service-related injury, he felt they still had a distance to go. Max did some research and learned that what we now call PTSD used to be regarded in the military as cowardice. Not that long ago, a soldier could even be shot for symptoms of PTSD. So there had been progress. On the other hand, PTSD had yet to be taken as seriously as other debilitating injuries. He joined the movement to qualify combat PTSD for award of the Purple Heart. Even the fact that there was such a cause helped him to better accept his own circumstances. The fact that others recognized a soldier's psychological wounds as deserving the same honor as physical wounds meant a lot to him. At this writing their cause is still pending as Max and others continue to press the military to recognize that not only are war wounds not shameful, they are *all* honorable, whether or not they can be seen.

Applications for You

It is at this point that I most regret that this is a book and that I cannot speak with you in person. That is because I very much believe in the power of human contact for healing and easing deep feelings of shame. So consider if there is one or more people you could possibly broach the subject with. A good question to start with is: Have you ever felt ashamed? If you first find out the other person has had a similar feeling of shame, it might pave the way for you to reveal your own.

However, before you approach anyone about your shame, please pay attention to this important caveat: It is not a good idea to dive right into a discussion or confession of shame. There is a danger you could feel even more ashamed if you have not carefully paved the way. You could suddenly find out your friend on the other end of the phone line has no time to talk with you right then—perhaps she is in the middle of a meeting or one of her kids requires immediate assistance. Or the friend you meet for lunch could have too much on his mind to give you the attention you need.

I confess to learning this the hard way. There is one particular situation that stands out. It was a hard lesson, but it taught me to take more care when approaching friends with difficult personal topics—ones difficult for me to talk about or for them to hear. That evening I was upset (though I do not remember why now) and the pressure in me to vent was strong. I met a friend for dinner. We had barely sat down when I blurted out my troubles, spilling them onto the table between us. I ranted on for about 5 minutes before realizing my friend was teary-eyed, staring slightly past my head. There was no contact there. The emotions that coursed through me simultaneously were strong. I was embarrassed not to have noticed my friend's state. Part of me felt ignored and I was angry. Then sadness filled me as I felt more alone than I had before attempting to say anything. It was a horrible feeling to so misjudge the situation. I finally pulled myself together to ask my friend what was wrong. It turned out he had just received very, very bad news and was more in need of my support than I was of his. I very much wished that I could turn back the clock so I could notice his distress right away and ask, "How are you?" before going on about me. It was after that evening that I vowed to always ask someone, "Is this a good time?" "Do you have a half hour now?" or some such before launching into anything that is precious to me. Actually, it is a good idea anytime and I have had more than one friend and colleague express appreciation for my consideration in asking. If the other person does not have time right then, ask them to make a date to meet or to call later.

It can be further helpful, once the other has assured you that the timing is good, to preface anything that could be potentially upsetting for them to hear, to give them the option to opt out. For example, on the topic of this key, you could say, "Would it be okay to talk with you about shame? It is something I'm grappling with and wonder if you ever have," or something like that. That way they are alerted to what they are signing on for. Some would criticize this idea as taking too much responsibility for the other person. I have a different way to look at it, though. I believe that by checking out the situation first I am actually taking very good care of me, bettering my chances to be heard. It helps me to ensure that when I finally share something that is very precious or difficult for me, the other person will be prepared to listen and stay in contact with me. You might try this idea with one or more friends and see if it is also useful for you.

This would also be a good situation for applying your mindful gauge (Key 1). First imagine talking with a selection of friends or family and see how your gauge reacts. You can decide who to talk with first, second, and so forth based on your gauge indicators.

Is This a Good Time for Addressing Your Shame?

Pay attention to timing. That is an important factor in many strategies and interventions, but particularly critical when dealing with shame. It would not be a good idea to push yourself prematurely into delving into shame. Use your mindful gauge to help you plan when a good time might be for dealing with one or another aspect of your shame. For some it will be best to approach shame toward the beginning of recovery; for others it should be a final stage. For you it may be somewhere in between. As with most every other aspect of recovery, timing for dealing with shame is individual. Just do not try to tackle it all at once. Here is a partial list of things you might consider before addressing your shame issues:

- Do you want to?
- Would there be any negative risks in resolving your shame?
- Can you get support for dealing with this, that is, one or more trusted individuals you can talk with?
- Do you have enough information about PTSD in general and typical consequences of your type of trauma in particular?

Exercise 1: The Value of Shame

Identify at least three positive functions for your feelings of shame in regard to your trauma. How has it alerted you to something being wrong? Has it helped to stop you from passing on harm to another? Perhaps it has made it possible for you to fit in better with your network or family. Add your discoveries into the material you will share with another. Do not be discouraged if nothing comes to mind. You can return to this exercise at a later date.

Exercise 2: Apportion Your Shame Fairly

Consider if, as in Eileen's case, there is someone else who should be bearing shame in your stead. Is it possible you have taken theirs on yourself? How can you (figuratively) assign their shame back to them, or at least relieve yourself of it? Use your mindful gauge to imagine scenarios or methods. Perhaps you will write a letter or poem, draw or paint a picture, or create a dialogue as if for a play. Whatever you do, keep in mind that the goal is to separate the other's shame from any that may legitimately be your own.

Exercise 3: Sharing Shame

Make a list of the things you are feeling ashamed of. Then organize your list, placing the ones that are the most difficult for you to face at the bottom and the ones that are least difficult (though of course none are easy) at the top. Choose one trusted friend or family member to tell about the *least* difficult shame. Starting there can build confidence and reduce overwhelm. Use the guidelines in the section Applications for You above to help you find the best person to talk with. Based on the result of your first trial, you can decide if you want to share more with that person or talk with another.

Evaluate This Key

The same guidelines apply for this key as for all the others. Is utilizing this key for you? What do your mindful gauge and common sense tell you?

Plan How to (or Not to) Use This Key

Has this key changed your relationship to your shame or to how you regard shame in general? How will such a shift in your thinking affect your perception of shame in yourself and others? Consider if there is any change and, if so, whether (or how) that will be useful as you go forward with your life. Are there any ways in which you can be alert for future encounters with shame in yourself, your family, or your friends?

KEY 6

TAKE SMALLER STEPS
FOR BIGGER LEAPS

It is better to take many small steps in the right direction than to make a great leap forward only to stumble backward. —CHINESE PROVERB

Moderation is the secret of survival. —MANLY HALL

My favorite book on the art of writing is Anne Lamott's *Bird by Bird: Some Instructions on Writing and Life*. It is a lovely little volume full of common sense and wisdom for writer and reader alike. A few pages into the first chapter, she recounts a family story that always proves helpful to her writing students. I include it here with the hope that her (and her father's) gentle wisdom may also be helpful to you in your trauma recovery:

> Thirty years ago my older brother, who was ten years old at the time, was trying to get a report on birds written that he'd had three months to write, which was due the next day. We were out at our family cabin in Bolinas, and he was at the kitchen table close to tears, surrounded by binder paper and pencils and unopened books on birds, immobilized by the hugeness of the task ahead. Then my father sat down beside him, put his arm around my brother's shoulder, and said, "Bird by bird, buddy. Just take it bird by bird." (pp. 18–19)

Are you overwhelmed by the task of your recovery? Or are you pushing too far or too fast and suffering rebound for your efforts? It is very, very common to be daunted by trauma healing and to want to hurry it, that is, go faster or take bigger steps than you are ready for. Who would not want to speed their way out of trauma? It feels awful. However, when you are paralyzed in the face of your goal or try to rush the process, the result can be frustration and relapse instead. It may seem too slow to tackle only one "bird" at a time, and manageable portions might seem like baby steps. But when you pare down each task to something you can actually accomplish, you better guarantee your eventual success. The Chinese proverb quoted above is a good reminder: It is better to take one seemingly absurdly small step that you can handle and succeed with safely than to overstretch your limits and risk backsliding or a worsening of your symptoms.

Of course, besides your own inner pressure, there are many circumstances that contribute to your impatience. Current insurance and employee assistance restrictions greatly interfere with finding your optimal portion and pace. They increasingly limit trauma therapy, sometimes to just a few sessions. Some of the self-help literature contributes to the impatience by promoting strategies that are claimed to be a quick fix. Add that to the pressure you feel just from living with trauma and PTSD itself and the result is not very pleasant; actually, when the helping agency or book is pushing you to recover more quickly than you are able to, the added stress can result in just the opposite. These situations can force traumatized individuals into attempting much bigger steps than they can really handle. When they bite off more than they can chew, the result can be a severe "indigestion" and recovery setback, sometimes a long way. This chapter will guide you toward better pacing, helping you to find the optimal stride for your system and situation.

Particularly when dealing with trauma, usually less is (really) more. Over the years I have noticed that the vast majority of supervision and consultation problems presented to me are solved by simply reducing the size of the steps being attempted. Of course that is not always easy for the individual or even a trauma therapist. Sometimes it is difficult for me to determine who is contributing most to the pressure, the helper or helpee. No matter—slowing them down is often difficult, though usually rewarding in the end.

Aiming for a step size that guarantees success—something you are sure you can do—is another helpful rule of thumb for trauma recovery. Actually it is a good standard when attempting most goals. Anne Lamott's father, in the story at the beginning of this chapter, illustrates the usefulness of this principle. His son was overwhelmed by the size of the project—all those birds! But he could write just a paragraph or two on *one* bird. Cutting that first step down to something he could achieve improved his chances of overall success. The same principle applies to trauma recovery. Building on small accomplishments not only moves you steadily toward healing, it also develops confidence and self-esteem. However, that means you have to carefully plan tasks that you can actually complete. Certainly there could be times you might want to attempt a goal that is a stretch. Just make sure the stretch is attainable, that you are fairly sure you can reach it. If not, pare it down a little to improve your chances. In general, success builds on success, increasing the chance of achieving more success.

Janice, discussed in Key 1, demonstrated the danger of setting goals beyond reach. She wanted to be hugged. Yet, when she leaped to that goal, she dissociated; it was too much. Though it was not easy for her, once she began to attempt smaller steps—having her friend simply place a hand on her shoulder was the first one—she succeeded. That first, small step led to others. Step by step, bird by bird, she became able to get (and give) a hug without disappearing or becoming frightened.

Learning to Swim

The following example illustrates a successful, if elementary, application of both principles discussed above.

Everyone knows that a nonswimmer should not begin in the deep end of the pool; to do so could prove fatal. At the least it would be overwhelmingly frightening, impeding potential progress. To learn to swim, we all must begin in the shallow end. And even there activities may need to be modified to ensure a pace we can manage.

My client Lilly was impatient with her 4-year-old, Meco. He loved his little, shallow play pool, but Lilly wanted him to learn to swim. It was an uphill battle; every time she took him in the big swimming pool, he would scream and cry. Obviously, being in the big pool was too scary for him, even with the security of holding onto her. I asked if she could minimize the challenge for him. Her level of frustration was blocking her clear thinking. She was unsure how to do it any differently. But she was open to ideas, so I suggested a possible first step: Have him merely sit on the side of the pool with his feet on the top step, just barely getting them wet. She agreed to try it. She came back the next week to report that it worked just fine. Meco liked to sit with only his feet in the water. I next suggested that Meco slide down to crouch—only on the first step—so his feet were wet and his buttocks would get a little wet. That went well too. The next week, he should sit on the first step with his feet on the second step. That way the lower half of his body would be in the water. By now Lilly had fully grasped the principle and reported at the next session that she had done as suggested one day, and then the next had also gotten Meco to crouch on the second step, getting wet up to his chest. They went on like that, one incremental challenge at a time. After 6 weeks, Meco was happy to be all the way in the pool in his mother's arms. Their next steps would involve developing actual swimming skills.

We solved Lilly and Meco's problem by reducing each progression to something that he could manage without fright—and even enjoy. At first it seemed ridiculously slow to Lilly, but looking back she was pleased with the result. Within a few months he was swimming like a fish. Of course it is possible that she could have just persisted in holding him in the water, telling him he was safe or getting irritated at his crying. Maybe eventually he would have tolerated it, but it could have hurt their bond. Reducing each task to something that was easy—and even enjoyable—resulted in success while preserving their (usually) good relationship.

The Value of Metered or Measured Avoidance

Sometimes reducing steps to manageable size may mean putting one or more steps aside, or changing them altogether, in the short or long term. Thirty-year-old Rosa had been neglected and physically abused as a child. Since her teens, she had panic attacks on a regular basis. Among her recovery goals was to stop the compulsion to cut her forearm. She often dissociated, and cutting was the way she would get back to feeling her body and reducing her fright. In discussing multiple possible strategies that might accomplish the same thing, I asked if she might try a cool shower—see if something less extreme could also work to get her back in touch. At this suggestion, Rosa's eyes widened. She paled and pulled her head back, inhaling sharply. Clearly, something I said had frightened her. After a short pause she told me that she was actually very afraid of taking showers. The shower terrified her. Nonetheless, the fact was that she took one nearly daily because there was no bathtub where she lived. It was not water she was afraid of, only the shower. Even though we were diverting to a seemingly different issue than her cutting, I wondered if they could be related. Moreover, I was very concerned that anyone with such a chronically high fear level would regularly be pushing herself to do something that frightened her further.

At this point I was not at all interested in *why* she was afraid of the shower. I assumed the origin had roots in the traumas she had suffered. However, it was not her history that was the priority here, but her present. Day-to-day living was extremely difficult, more so because of her fear of the shower. For that reason, I did not want to discuss her past, which could risk a worsening of symptoms when decreasing symptoms was the most important.

In discussing this with Rosa, she was in agreement that showering was not particularly good for her emotionally, but she could see no other option for reasons of hygiene. I asked if she would consider an alternative for a temporary trial if we were able to find a suitable substitute. She was eager to hear my idea. Since Rosa was not afraid of water, nor the bathroom or kitchen sinks, I asked if she could sponge bathe and wash her hair in one basin or the other. She was intrigued with the idea and wondered if her high stress had prevented her from think-ing of it herself. Yes, she would like to try that substitute. She set a goal for 3 weeks.

We continued to meet as we tracked Rosa's response to avoiding the shower. The worst part of the experiment for her was a mild embarrassment that she was not showering "like everyone else." She felt a bit of a coward. On the bright side, her chronic level of fear reduced considerably and the episodes of dissociation decreased noticeably. Because she was not dis-sociating so often or so severely, she was also cutting less. All in all, it was a very successful experiment for her.

Though she was tempted to give up showers forever, social conformity won out and she decided to go back to showering at least a few times a week. When she did, she found something else had changed—she was significantly less afraid. She still did not particularly like to shower, but since she had gained an alternative, it no longer caused her to panic or dissociate. Par-ticularly on days that her anxiety was already quite high, she would opt to bathe in the sink. Though drastically reduced in frequency and severity, Rosa was still cutting herself from time to time. Eliminating that completely remained a goal. But because of her bathing success, she now saw that as an attainable goal, knowing she just had to find the necessary steps and pace.

Apply a Little Theory

I have struggled a bit with this section of this chapter because the concept of this key, taking smaller steps, is not scientific. There is no actual research to support that this strategy will help you. However, it *is* common sense, which sometimes is more accurate than science. Moreover, most would agree that manageable pacing is necessary for a course of healing from any malady to be successful. For example, even though treatment for cancer needs to be quick and strong to save lives, sometimes a course of chemotherapy needs to be slowed or paused to allow the patient's body to survive the cure. If a step is too big to manage or be successful, it must be trimmed to an achievable size. The old Chinese proverb on this chapter's first page says it all. When a big leap—no matter how attractive—will land you in worse trouble than when you started, you must resize your steps.

Of course you get impatient. You want to recover now, yesterday even. Remember: Your own pace, the one that will actually get you to your goal—even if it seems slow—is the one to choose. Do you remember Aesop's Fables? His stories have been popular for 1,500 years because they contain timeless common sense and wisdom. One of his best-known fables, the story about the *Tortoise and the Hare*, is a relevant example here. The lesson of the story rings true for trauma recovery as well as many other situations: "Slow and steady wins the race"— or, in the case of trauma healing, makes for a much better chance for recovery.

Traumatized individuals often have huge, overwhelming goals. Beth fell into this category. She knew what she wanted but was at a loss for how she could even begin to reach her objectives. She aimed "to have a better life," which is a worthy, though huge goal with many elements and steps involved. So to narrow the immediate task, I asked her what would be a first step toward her better life. "To have more money." Still too big to work with concretely, so I asked again. What would be the first step toward having more money? "To feel better about myself." And the first step toward that? And so on. In this way Beth reduced and focused the first step to a smaller, more precise size. I kept notes so that we had a record of each aim, in case she wanted to revisit any of them. Finally I asked her, "What step you could take *today* toward your objective?" Finally she was able to zero in on an attainable, concrete goal: "I need more backbone—literally. I need to feel stronger in my back. Sometimes I don't feel like I can hold myself up!" It was the first time she had stated (and understood) a clear, simple aim. She believed that her lack of backbone handicapped her in many areas, also in the business world. Helping her improve in that area might have long-range effects. So that is exactly what we proceeded to do, to physically build strength in her back muscles to give her a better sense of "backbone" and to better hold herself up. Beth also came up with homework that included regular exercise (see the next key, "Get Moving") and consulting a physical therapist. Looking back a few months later, she reflected that strengthening her backbone had been an invaluable first step. It had given her a concrete foundation to build upon as she took further steps toward her goal of a better life.

The Case and the Key

In the mid-1980s, Gary contacted me to help his dying wife. Our first contacts were on her behalf at their home. While visiting with her, I observed his high level of anxiety and emotional exhaustion, but he always insisted that it was she who needed my help. Even so, after a few months, he called and asked if I would talk with him too. He agreed that it would not be optimal at his house as he needed to discuss and express his feelings about impending loss and daily overwhelm. But there was a big problem in his coming to my 18th floor office: He was terribly afraid of both elevators and heights. He did not think he would be able to come up to my workplace, at least not in any shape to be able to make use of my professional help.

As a compromise, for several weeks Gary and I had sessions on the telephone when his wife was sleeping. Sometimes he went out to a pay phone using the excuse of running errands (this was before the advent of mobile telephones). Of course neither alternative was particularly optimal and Gary began to be frustrated by his limitations. More than once he expressed a longing to overcome his fears and meet me at my office. After a while, I suggested that perhaps we could negotiate a meeting at my building on a lower floor. He was interested in the idea, if a bit skeptical. So I suggested that he use his mindful gauge (see Key 1) while imagining different scenarios and see if any felt comfortable enough to try. After reviewing several circumstances, Gary came up with a possibility: If I would ride with him in the elevator, he thought he could make it up eight floors, to the building coffee shop. It was mostly free of customers in the middle of the afternoon. Gary imagined that we might sit in a corner away from the windows so we would be able to talk comfortably. He was willing to try it and so was I.

Gary was a bit embarrassed to need such a special consideration, though he wanted to find a better situation for utilizing my help. The first time we rode up in the elevator from the lobby to the eighth floor, he was quite nervous. The second time less so. On each subsequent occasion of riding the elevator, Gary became more comfortable. Once in the coffee shop, sitting away from the windows was always fine, never a problem. However, though no one ever sat near enough to us to hear our conversation, the periodic traffic in and out of the café was sometimes distracting. But we made the most of it.

We met that way for several weeks. Then, toward the end of one session, Gary asked if I would take him up to the 18th floor. He just wanted to try the long trip in the elevator and then come right down again. Of course I agreed. The following week, he asked if he could see where my office was, just in the hall, not walking inside or near a window. Sure, no problem. The next time we were talking in the coffee shop, I asked him what he might need to be able to actually come into my office. If I would close the blinds so he could not see how high up he was, he might be able to manage. So the next week we went up to my floor and walked into my rather dark office, blinds fully closed ahead of time.

We talked there for a few minutes, but I could see Gary's distress rising. He agreed that he was getting anxious, but he did not want to give in to it. I reassured him that he had taken a very big step that day and strongly advised that we go back down to the coffee shop for the rest of the session. Once there, Gary calmed, but he remained frustrated that it had been necessary to return to the café; it felt like a step backward to him. I disagreed. I pointed out that he was only looking at what he had not done, and not the huge step forward he had made, actually coming up to the 18th floor and sitting for a while in my office. I was genuinely proud of him. My perspective helped him to accept that all in all, he had been more successful than not. Over the next few weeks we spent increasing periods of time in my office, always ending at the coffee shop. Eventually we stayed for the whole time. On that occasion Gary was really proud of himself, too.

For both of us, it was a relief to meet regularly in the privacy of my office. Gary was thrilled at his success and at the greater freedom to talk openly. He soon suggested that I not meet him in the lobby anymore, but on the eighth floor at the coffee shop. It took only 2 weeks before he was riding all the way up to my office on his own. And then a few weeks later he got up while we were talking, walked over to the blinds, and peeked out. Just once, but he did it completely on his own. After that, during each session he would open the blinds and look out the window for gradually longer periods of time. One day he surprised me by leaving the blinds open as he returned to his chair. Though it had never really been a goal of the therapy, Gary cured his fear of heights. The key had clearly been sizing the increments so that he could manage each step, building one on another. His success boosted his confidence to face the impending loss of his wife and huge changes in his life. "If I can conquer my fear of heights, I can do anything!" he bravely asserted. Of course he faced difficult times ahead, but he was correct that his accomplishment did increase his resilience.

Imagine how it would have been for Gary had he pushed himself to come up to my office prematurely. I suspect he would have had a panic or anxiety attack and been discouraged from trying it again. By negotiating manageable steps, he conquered two phobias: elevators and heights. Considering he was in his 70s and had been plagued by those fears for most of his life, it was a huge victory for him. Smaller steps "won the race."

Applications for You

If you are having difficulty reaching one or more of your goals, the key to your own success may lie in taking one "bird" at a time or breaking down your steps into smaller bits. The more concretely you can do them, the better. Do not be afraid to begin with one or more steps that seem ridiculously tiny, or to attempt the easiest step first. Remember, you have Aesop ("The Tortoise and the Hare"), Anne Lamott (*Bird by Bird*), and a wealth of common sense behind you.

Probably the only contraindication for using this key is if it does not make sense to you. However, even if it does make sense and you want to apply it, you could receive objections from friends, family, or a helping professional. Years ago my therapist cautioned me against slowing down my recovery process. To be honest, I was both threatened by and appalled at his attitude. At that point in time I could not think of anything more contrary to my progress than being pushed. Though it was difficult for me to do so, I insisted, asserting my opinion and taking responsibility for the outcome. "If it takes longer and costs me more money, so be it," I told him. But I really believed that slowing things down and taking more control, myself, would speed things up in the long run. This is the kind of thing that there is no way to really evaluate, except by your own judgment and common sense. I chose the slower path and it was successful for me. I do not know what would have happened if I had succumbed to my therapist's pressure. There might also have been a good outcome. However, at the time (and still when I look back), the speed he was advocating just seemed, and felt, wrong. I have never regretted asserting my right to my own pace.

Exercise 1: Practice Reducing a Step to Smaller Steps

Choose something you do on a daily basis: washing dishes, laundry, cooking, and so on. Write down the task and then break it down into the steps involved. Look over the list and see if any of the steps can be further reduced. It may be a tedious exercise, but it will give you practice using something benign before moving on to something more critical. It will also help to reinforce the idea that any task can be broken down into smaller steps.

Exercise 2: Bird by Bird

Make a list of your goals for trauma recovery. Make a check mark by each of the ones you have been attempting at the same time. Then go back and give each of those goals a priority number (1, 2, 3, etc.), paying attention to ones that are prerequisites to others. Then revise the list in order, putting the ones that need attention first at the top and the ones that are less urgent, or need to be addressed later, toward the bottom. Then start at the top of your list, strategizing for how you will tackle that first "bird" on its own.

Exercise 3: Step Down a Goal

- From your list of goals, above, choose one.
- On a piece of paper, list as many steps as you can think of toward that goal. Leave several lines in between each step.
- Highlight the steps you can take or have already taken.
- Choose one step you have not yet accomplished to focus on first. Then list several steps toward that single step.
- Keep reducing steps until you have one you can accomplish today (as in the example of Beth above).

Exercise 4: Temporarily Remove or Replace an Upsetting Task

Like Rosa, do you have something you must do on a daily or regular basis that causes you extreme distress? If so, see if it is possible to give yourself a break from it. For instance, do you panic taking the subway to work? Perhaps you could walk, ride the bus, or even take a taxi for a short period of time. You might need to allow extra time, but it could be worth it to experiment— or at the least to know you have a choice.

Of course if what troubles you is something you cannot avoid, such as, for example, sleep, the challenge will be to find a different way to do it, one that reduces the stress. Continuing with sleep as an illustration, finding out what it is that frightens you could give the clue to intervention. If it is the dark, perhaps sleeping with a light on would change something. If it could be the bedroom, moving to the living room or den couch for a while could help. The bottom line is to change anything that gives you a greater sense of control over your circumstances, including your distressing symptoms.

Evaluate This Key

How does this principle of taking smaller steps suit you? Which of my suggestions appeal to you and which do not? How would you alter those ideas or exercises that are not useful to you to something that is useful? Have you applied your mindful gauge to help you decide which exercises to attempt? If not, this may be a good time to review the first key to reinforce the usefulness of that too.

Plan How to (or Not to) Use This Key

In which areas would it be good for you to focus on taking smaller steps? How will you continue to identify where you need to reduce step size? What will signal you have bitten off more than you can chew? Might you use your mindful gauge to predict steps that might be too much? Plan ahead by writing down a goal and predicting the steps, then identifying substeps to each of them.

KEY 7

GET MOVING

I think if I were you, in case my mind were not exactly right, I would avoid being idle.

—ABRAHAM LINCOLN, letter to friend Joshua Speed, February 13, 1842

Movement is a medicine for creating change in a person's physical, emotional, and mental states. —CAROL WELCH

Firefighters, police, and the military—those whose daily work involves the highest incidence of stress and trauma—know that exercise and keeping fit are necessary to counteract the persistent strain and upset of their work. (And I appreciate being reminded of this often when I go for walks at the Santa Monica beach, where the local fire department sends their crew to jog—they are inspiring as well as lovely to watch.) These experts have a lot to teach us about managing the effects of traumatic stress. Their experience could be useful to you as well: Carefully chosen physical activity will make a meaningful contribution to your recovery from trauma.

There is a medical term for the trend in Western civilization toward less and less physical activity: sedentary lifestyle. It has become a general problem, at the root of increasing rates of obesity, heart disease, and other (often) preventable conditions. The benefits of exercise for physical health have been studied widely. Its application to reducing depression has a significant body of research. Less explored, but no less important is the potential for activity and exercise to relieve the symptoms associated with trauma and PTSD. Just about everyone I have worked with has benefited. However, most have also begun reluctantly.

Jack comes to mind first. He was not long out of college when I first saw him. He was thin and frail, and still suffering greatly from his childhood. The worst of his traumas included his mother's regular bouts of physical abuse and bullying by several schoolmates. In his early 20s, day-to-day life was difficult for him. He was lucky to find work that demanded little of him while providing a nominal income and a daily structure. He sought me out with great hopes that I might instantly cure his ills and set him on his life path.

The major thing that struck me about Jack was his obvious physical weakness. He was pale, slouched, and had very little muscle tone anywhere on his body; his clothes hung off bones. I could not imagine how he would withstand the rigors of his life, let alone the demands of trauma therapy. Simultaneous to addressing emotional issues, I strongly recommended he begin an exercise regime. Specifically, I counseled that increasing his muscle strength through weight training might help him feel stronger in mind as well as body. His youth was a great advantage and lent him a level of enthusiasm that was an ally to his recovery. After a short period of skepticism, he took to physical exercise like a fish to water, such a natural at it that I wondered why he or someone else had not thought of it before. He loved lifting weights and marveled at the evidence of success he could see in the mirror from week to week as his physique developed. Alongside his bigger muscles, his psychological state began to stabilize and his courage to increase. One day he astonished me with the announcement that since he had so much more energy, he had taken a more challenging job at a higher wage. He proudly insisted that we increase his nominal fee.

This may all sound like a miracle, but it was also a lot of hard work on Jack's part. He had to structure his life differently to fit in the exercise program he designed for himself. That included devoting less time to television at night so he could get to bed early and get up early. The trainer at his gym coached him in nutrition. Jack took on his physical improvement as the primary project in his life.

Of course his improved condition did not solve his childhood problems. But it did change his relationship to them as his current life improved. What was going on *now* became his priority; feelings about then became less acute. After about a year and a half, he decided he did want to talk about what had happened to him as a child. By then his stability was so improved physically and emotionally (see Phase I in Key 3) that I was very willing to accompany him down that road (Phase II).

Most of you reading this book will not need or achieve the level of bodybuilding that Jack did. However, each of you will likely gain something useful if you get moving. Just make sure to plan your program with an eye to appropriate exercise and activity tailored to your own body's capabilities and limitations and your emotional needs.

The Issue

Moving—exercise and fitness—as it applies to safe recovery from trauma has at least three potential benefits:

1. As an antidote to a persistent freeze response
2. To increase containment and self-control via increased muscle tone
3. To dissipate buildup of stress hormones and help regulate ongoing stress levels

As An Antidote to a Persistent Freeze Response

People often bog down in the aftermath of trauma. As discussed previously, they often get stuck in the past. In addition, they can become fixated on their bodies. Symptoms of posttraumatic stress tend to be very unpleasant, even paralyzing. In the aftermath of trauma it is tempting to pull in, to reduce the amount and scope of activity. Trauma can make it difficult to go to work or even get out of bed. Of course, when physical injury is involved, that must be addressed first. But when the lasting impairment is primarily psychological, as is the norm with PTSD, physical symptoms may still be plentiful. To get moving reinforces the epilogue (see Key 2) by sending an active, nonverbal message to the body and the mind that there is no longer a need to freeze, or that the freeze response has ceased, because the trauma is over.

When Kate's house was burglarized in the middle of the night, her husband quietly called the police and then snuck downstairs with a baseball bat to confront the robbers. Kate knew what was happening, but was frozen with fear, unable to move from her bed throughout the entire incident. She wanted to hold her husband back from confronting them but was unable to move or utter a sound. Luckily the police arrived quickly and no one got hurt. The burglars were apprehended. However, 2 years later, Kate remained housebound, afraid to go out. The only excursions she could tolerate were quick grocery trips and other short errands. Her body had become stiff with chronic remnants of the paralysis she experienced the night of the attempted robbery. And her husband was worried about (and frustrated with) her.

Kate was not willing to come to my office, so at first I made home visits. We worked with various strategies, most contributing to improvement. However, it turned out to be simple physical exercise that helped her make the biggest strides. Of course she would not go to a local gym. But she was willing to increase her activity at home. They bought a treadmill and Kate began to walk daily, building up to several miles over a few months. Gradually she added other physical activities, including stretching and push-ups.

The exercise helped her to feel more in control again and

she became interested in fixing up the garden. That actually gave her a huge boost as she spent several hours most days with soil and plants. She reminded me what good therapy gardening can be for many people. One night as she had a repeating nightmare about the burglary, something in it changed. Instead of the usual dream of being frozen in her bed, she found herself on the stairs with a shovel in her hands. When one of the robbers came near, she whacked him with it. For the first time in 2 years she woke with a smile on her face.

Kate still had some distance to go in resolving the burglary trauma and getting her life back on track, but she had made great strides. Physically intervening in chronic freeze had shifted something deep inside her. Both the exercise and the gardening were important. A few months later she decided to take a self-defense class to increase her confidence and sense of security. Though she hoped her home would never be burglarized again, if there was a next time she wanted to be able to really smash the offender with a shovel.

To Increase Containment and Self-control via Increased Muscle Tone

Muscle tension is an underrated ally. While relaxation can be valuable at times, without muscle tension you would be unable to stand, walk, sit, or hold this book in your hands. Tension helps us complete the tasks of daily life; without it we would be immobile. Of course there are degrees of tension that can be unpleasant and even cause difficulty—like almost anything else, the extremes of tension, particularly chronic tension, are not particularly helpful. Though most people would assume relaxation is the state that helps trauma recovery most, a good portion of traumatized individuals do not do well with relaxation. In a relaxed state, they may actually become more anxious or even panicked.

Jack and Kate, above, are good examples of this exact problem. When I first met them, they both were out of control of their anxiety. Jack had tried listening to relaxation CDs and Kate was attempting *progressive relaxation*. However, neither of them was helped by loosening up. In fact, Kate's symptoms actually worsened when she was practicing the relaxation method. The strategy that turned the tide for each of them was increasing the tone of their muscles. When they were physically stronger, they became emotionally stronger as well.

To Dissipate Buildup of Stress Hormones and Help Regulate Ongoing Stress Levels

Sports and aerobic exercise help us blow off steam. And with that steam dissipates a portion of stress hormones. This is a main reason that those with highly stressful work, as mentioned above, will run, play football, or work out vigorously and so on. A growing body of research continues to underscore the value of exercise in reducing the effects of stress. It does this through several actions. One of the results is an increase in endorphins, those brain chemicals that make us feel good. Another is a reduction in chronic adrenaline levels as the exertion uses it up.

There is a caution here, however: Not all trauma survivors are able to make use of strenuous exercise. Some may need to engage at a lower level of activity, at least at first. The traumatic stress reaction increases heart rate and breathing, so activities that do likewise can trigger flashbacks in some traumatized individuals. That is not helpful. For them, beginning with exercise that does not increase pulse and respiration is the better tactic. Slow, purposeful weight training, beginning with light weights (including milk cartons and the like), can be a good starting point. See my own story, below, for more on this principle.

The most important thing is for you to find the type of exercise that improves your situation. Using your mindful gauge as well as common sense will help you to identify what is best for your body, your mind, and your circumstances.

The Case

My own PTSD had roots in a couple of childhood incidents. For the most part, through my teens and college years, I was unaware of the impact those incidents had and would have on me. There were minor bouts with stress or anxiety, including some insomnia in high school. But for the most part, my life moved forward fairly normally. However, in my early 30s, I began to have increasing trouble, including the development of panic attacks. This peaked at the beginning of the 1980s when PTSD was a new and rare diagnosis. The therapists I sought help from at that time had never heard of it and neither had I. No one understood why I was having so much trouble dealing with my feelings and everyday life. As my difficulties increased with regular bouts of anxiety and panic, my life became more and more restricted. Soon I had added agoraphobia to the mix of my difficulties. I was not quite housebound, but increasingly limited in what I dared to do. Even trips to the grocery store became a major emotional challenge. Typical of PTSD, I felt out of control of my mind, my body, and my life. Many factors were involved in the breakdown of my emotional and mental systems. It took several years and a variety of strategies to get me fully back to myself. Perhaps I will write about my whole experience in a memoir someday. But in this chapter, I want to focus on the central role that getting myself moving played in beginning and sustaining my own recovery from trauma.

Apply a Little Theory

When you get moving, you will be accomplishing at least two important goals for trauma recovery: Counteracting any lingering freeze response in your system and increasing the capacity of your body to contain the arousal of the traumatic stress response. In this section, we will look at the theory that underlies these important interventions.

Counteracting Freeze

While often a lifesaver (as discussed in Key 5A, "Forgive Your Limitations"), freezing in response to trauma has consequences. In fact, it is believed that dissociative reactions, including freezing, during a traumatic incident predict PTSD. That is to say, those who freeze rather than fight or flee have the greatest possibility for developing long-term problems. So if you have PTSD, it is likely you froze during one or more traumas.

The freezing reaction can continue to be triggered after a trauma is over via flashbacks. Something in the internal or external environment serves to remind your amygdala (see Key 1) of the trauma and the reaction is set in motion. One strategy for countering habitual paralysis is to train yourself to move — even if only a little — whenever you freeze. A movement as simple as standing up, walking a few steps, or even just lifting your finger or arm a few inches can break the freezing "spell." When I am working with people who are or become frozen, I will ask them to wiggle their fingers or even to look at the clock, just to get them moving. Such a minor intervention sends a powerful message to the amygdala that the trauma is actually over because now you can move.

The Body's Container

Muscular relaxation (e.g., via massage, yoga, stretching, soft furniture) is a frequent goal of stressed-out people. Of course that can be ideal for many. But for a good portion of those suffering traumatic stress, the value of relaxation is highly overrated, even misleading. A number of you reading this now may already have noticed that the more relaxed you get, the more nervous you become. It is possible you have not told anyone because you thought something was wrong with you. I hope it will be a relief for you to know this is a common reaction in those with PTSD and also persons with anxiety and panic problems. A full 4% of the general population is believed to get more anxious from attempts at relaxation, though it is not possible to translate that into the exact numbers of those with PTSD.

This unexpected phenomenon can be particularly (and frustratingly) demonstrated at bedtime. A common scenario finds the exhausted trauma survivor lying in bed dazed by the amount of anxious energy coursing through her body. What happened? She was ready to sleep, but as soon as she relaxed and started to drift off, her body became highly agitated and uncomfortable. All of a sudden she was completely awake with no hope of sleep—another cycle of insomnia had begun. For some of these traumatized insomniacs, attempting a gentle muscle tensing before sleep will help to contain the stress arousal just enough to allow sleep.

No one is really sure why increasing muscle tone helps people with PTSD; however, we can speculate. In part, any benefit will depend on where in your body you increase tone. For example, increasing tension in the legs, feet, and back may improve your balance and ability to hold yourself up. More tone across your chest or back can help you to feel more protection—armor—between yourself and others.

A particularly emotionally fragile Danish client, Tina, had difficulty at large family gatherings where a buffet lunch was the traditional norm. Every time she went to the food table, with her back to the room and the other people, she would become so nervous she could not fill her plate. She rarely ate much at those gatherings. Even more problematic was her increasing emotional discomfort. She considered giving up going to gatherings altogether.

In reviewing the scenario with her mindful gauge, Tina was able to identify that it was an extreme feeling of vulnerability that made her so uncomfortable turning her back to her family. Neither of us had ever encountered such a problem before, so we agreed to just experiment and see what, if anything, might help her. Through trial and error we discovered that having Tina tense the area between her shoulder blades, by pulling them toward each other, significantly reduced the vulnerable feeling. However, by pulling her shoulders back, she felt too exposed in her chest. More experimentation led to a rather awkward pose involving pulling together her shoulder blades while simultaneously tipping the upper edges of her shoulders forward and down. Admittedly, it was a bit weird. But it worked. In that position Tina felt like she had on a suit of armor, that she was protected. If she could maintain the necessary posture, she believed she would be able to get something to eat. I suggested that the more she practiced, the easier and more subtle the necessary tensions would become. And over a few weeks' time it did become more automatic for her. At the next family reunion, she was able to get a plate of food without emotional difficulty, even if she did still feel a bit stiff in her movements. The experiment was successful.

A plastic bottle of soda helps to illustrate my hypothesis for why muscle tensing helps emotional containment. I figure that the soda is under pressure inside its flexible container, which is somewhat akin to the kind of pressure that is inside the body and musculature of a person with PTSD. If the bottle is too soft, the pressurized pop contents will not be well contained. They could leak all over the place. I see a parallel to trauma-pressurized people; their container also needs to be firm like the plastic soda bottle, to keep the pressure of their traumatic stress in check and manageable. Muscle tone increases the firmness.

Discovering My Key

Because I felt so vulnerable, I knew that any exercise would have to be graduated, starting simple, easy, and slow to avoid aerobic stimulation. If I could just build up without increasing my heart rate, that would be ideal. Further, I would have to do it at home, as going to a gym would be an over-the-top challenge. For me to be able to succeed at this, I would have to make it safe for my then-fragile psyche.

I made two investments: a pad of graph paper and a very cheap set of free weights. I used the graph paper to plot a program. Down the left side I listed my starting exercises: bicep curls, side leg lifts, back leg lifts, wall push-ups, and barbell lifts. Across the top I used one tiny square for each day I would "work out," putting the dates along the top. I started with three days per week. I wrote work out in quotes above because I could not really call it that. The first day I only did about three repetitions of each activity: three curls, three lifts with each leg, three wall push-ups, and so on. I did not dare to do more for fear of raising my pulse. However, I did each one and recorded the number of repetitions on the graph paper. It was a relief just to do something proactive. Two days later I did four repetitions of each exercise. Every subsequent exercise day I would increase the number of repetitions by one. It seemed pitifully little to do and slow to build. But the fact remained that I was doing *something*. And I was moving my body without triggering panic. On the contrary, fairly quickly I discovered that my stress level was less and my breathing was easier immediately following the exercises. Gradually I began to see slight improvements in my stability when I was at home and when I went out. Do not misunderstand me—this was not a quick miracle cure. I do not remember exactly, but it probably took a year before I was back to mostly normal activities. But fairly early on I could see that using and building up my muscles was having a positive, if very slow, effect.

Since that time, exercise remains a loyal friend. In fact, I am sure it is one of the ways I continue to manage the stress of my life and the growth of my career. During my years living and working in Denmark, walking was my major means of transportation. I also began regular swimming while living there. Today, back home in Los Angeles, I exercise regularly, including swimming and walking. Over the years I have become convinced that my mental health and physical health are intertwined, so I do what I can to support both.

Applications for You

What helped me back then was the combination of structured activity (recorded on my graph paper) and a gradual buildup of muscle tone. Those may help you, or it may be something quite different. How you get moving must be tailored to your needs, body, mind, and situation. Perhaps walking or taking a Pilates class will be best for you; maybe weights or jogging. Do not be limited by my examples or exercises—please think outside the book. What is good for your friend may not be good for you and vice versa. Though I could not manage aerobic exercise when I had PTSD, you might do well with it. Use your mindful gauge to imagine different ways you might get moving and choose experiments based on the responses of your gauge. Then try a little of whatever seems most likely and evaluate again before settling on your plan.

It will be important to work your personal program into some kind of a routine or schedule. Regular activity at a level you can manage well will quickly become self-rewarding. There is a common wisdom about exercise: Once you get into the habit of it, the longer you keep at it, the easier it becomes to keep up. The rewards build and will help you to stay active once you have gotten over the first few humps.

Before You Begin

There are criteria to consider before committing to an exercise program, including the following:

- Desire. Though obviously I hope you will, you must pay attention to whether you want to get moving or not. It may seem silly that I even remind you of this. However, it is so easy for a reader to just follow the expert's advice. And I honestly do not think that is a good idea. Any step you take for your recovery must be something you want to do and see the value of. Do not let me or anyone else seduce you into doing something you do not want to or believe would be wrong for you.

- Health. Make sure your doctor approves any exercise program.
- Time. You need to set aside or make time for your activities.
- Money. If you want to do something that has a fee—joining a gym, taking Pilates classes, and so on—make sure you can afford it.
- Location. Consider if you will be best off at home or going out.

Exercise 1: Find Your Activity

Imagine different types of exercise: walking, jogging, types of weight lifting, sit-ups, push-ups, Pilates, yoga, step class, bicycling, treadmill, and anything else you can think of. You might start by imagining one or two, or go through a whole list at one time. Make sure you only attempt a portion you can manage. Then use your mindful gauge to identify which—if any—you would actually like to experiment with. Then arrange to try them one at a time. When sampling, make sure to apply your mindful gauge as well as common sense to each to find which is best for you at this time. Remember to include options such as team sports, gardening, and so on, anything that involves physical exertion or increasing strength. It could be a bonus if you find something to do with others, giving you contact at the same time you build your physical and emotional stability.

Exercise 2: Set Up Record Keeping

Would a log help you to maintain a regular schedule of activity? If so, what would work for you? For me it was a graph, but for you it may be something different. Would you like to buy small stars or other types of stickers to record your progress? Or maybe you will put an amount of money in a can each time you exercise, then use the collection for a big treat. Anything that would supportively encourage you to keep at it is fair to try.

Exercise 3: Find an Exercise Buddy

Remember that contact and support are also important factors for your recovery. Exercise and sports can be a source of companionship. For many, exercising and sticking with an activity program is easier and more fun when done together with a friend or acquaintance. Consider who you know who either is already exercising or could use help getting up and out. If you are not ready to exercise together with another, you could still have support through regular phone or e-mail contact reporting on or discussing your get moving program. In that way you might also support someone else who needs to get moving (see Key 8, "Make Lemonade").

Evaluate This Key

This might be one of the easier keys for you to evaluate as many of your reactions, positive and negative, will be highly physical and relatively immediate. Have you found the right activity? Is the effect purely physical, or can you also see an impact in other areas: emotions, outlook, and such?

Plan How to (or Not to) Use This Key

If you find you are not doing your set exercise program, refer back to the chapter on smaller steps (Key 6). It is likely you have tried too much or begun too soon. Reduce the amount or rene-gotiate your timing. Keep adjusting until you find something you can and will do and stick with. Remember, I had to start with just three repetitions of a mere handful of exercises. Even if it is only one, that could be the right place for you to start.

MAKE LEMONADE

Isn't it grand what an oyster can do with a morsel of sand?
What couldn't we do if we'd only begin
With some of the things that get under our skin.   —AUTHOR UNKNOWN

A good exercise for the heart is bending down and helping someone to get up.
                                                                —PROVERB

"When life gives you lemons make lemonade" is a catch-phrase that has come to stand for turning life's adversity into benefit for yourself or others. To make lemonade means to rise above the lousy hand you were dealt, making the best of it and helping others despite or in spite of it. My colleague and friend, Linda Lowitz, practices this principle on a daily basis. For many years she has been wheelchair bound with crippling rheumatoid arthritis—the most severe form. It came on gradually, increasingly degrading her mobility and quality of life. She watched her independence disappear as she lost many abilities, finally giving in to the need for a wheelchair over a decade ago. Nevertheless she has always kept her faith in life, her sense of humor, and her desire to help others. Throughout her physical decline, she maintained her job at the Los Angeles Department of Veterans Affairs where she worked as a social worker helping traumatized veterans. As she became ever more disabled, she adjusted her office and transportation to make it possible to continue, becoming a recognized and well-respected figure rolling around the VA. Even in retirement, she continues to advocate for the rights of the disabled, particularly in the schools. When I picture the concept of making lemonade, it is Linda Lowitz who first comes to my mind.

An important aspect of recovery for many of you will be to find a meaning in your experience that can turn at least some of your tragedy into benefit, at least for you and perhaps also for others. However, *when* you add making lemonade to your recovery process will depend on timing and your own abilities and circumstances. When reeling in the immediate aftermath of trauma, few are in a frame of mind or body to consider how such an experience could have any beneficial aspects. By inclusion of this key, I do not, in any way, make light of trauma—remember, I have had PTSD; I have also been in your shoes. However, if this idea is either a turnoff or premature for your situation, skip this key or postpone it to a more appropriate time for you.

How you make lemonade will depend on many factors, including timing. In some circumstances, such as when trauma hits an entire family, neighborhood, or community, lending help to others can (and should) be done right away. Whatever you can do for others who are going through the same thing as you (e.g., earthquake, flood, shooting) will also help you. The ways in which many acutely traumatized people helped each other following the terrorism of September 11, 2001, and Hurricane Katrina are good examples. In general, those who jump in to help fare much better in the long term than those who do not. In other instances, making lemonade may need to be postponed until you are further through your recovery or even wait until you are fully recovered. Your mindful gauge and common sense can be helpful to you in determining if, how, and when to make lemonade.

My own situation may serve as another example. PTSD knocked me down for several years, shaking me to my core. Making lemonade never even crossed my mind. I struggled on a daily basis to meet my basic needs and obligations. Eventually I was able to make lemonade through my professional activities and through writing books. Admittedly, I did not set out consciously to do that. That was not my deliberate intention. My formulated viewpoint and writing came later. In the beginning I was reacting, sometimes angrily, to the many misguided steps and unhelpful interventions I had endured in the years when no one really knew how to help someone with trauma. I channeled my anger toward figuring out what went wrong and what I found helpful. My goal gradually focused on making trauma recovery easier on others than it had been on me. For the most part, I had been pushed prematurely into overwhelming processes with no checks or balances to slow down or stop once the process had been set in motion. Years later as I delved into studying trauma (theory, history, treatments) and began to lecture, many people came forward to tell me of similar experiences—of their own and others they knew. Some of these individuals suffered periods of (or even permanent) severe dysfunction as a result of improper or insufficient treatment. Because of the multitude of such known incidents (I suspect there are also many that never come to light) I became determined to better educate those who have been traumatized, giving them solid information and a greater number of recovery options and strategies. I have also endeavored to contribute to the knowledge and tools of trauma professionals. That is how I have made (and continue making) lemonade from my trauma lemons. In this, I am not alone. There are truly many who have made lemonade from their trauma, including most of my colleagues who specialize in helping others to recover from trauma. Just about every professional I have met who specializes in the field of traumatic stress has experienced trauma themselves—I think of us as a profession of wounded healers.

In addition, everyday people are turning their adversity into advantage. Helping or advocating for others is a frequent way that traumatized individuals make lemonade with their trauma lemons. Organizations such as Mothers Against Drunk Driving (MADD), the Reach to Recovery volunteers from the American Cancer Society, the television series *America's Most Wanted*, the Matthew Shepard Foundation, and the Amber Alert Program all resulted from trauma survivors turning their rotten experiences into help for others. They each made lemonade from their tragedy and made it possible for other people to become active and do the same. Also, it is important to note that there are people everywhere making lemonade without becoming famous. They are helping neighbors, friends, and family, volunteering to help the elderly, children, the homeless, and getting involved in political campaigns and community projects.

What you eventually do may or may not be directly connected to your trauma. Of course you will need to take care not to jump into something that actually makes you feel worse, triggers flashbacks, or the like. Make sure what you do decreases your symptoms. If you become worse, you will need to find something else. Timing is also an important consideration. It would not be wise to feel pushed by the message of this chapter into jumping in too quickly or doing too much. If you feel unable to go out, you might begin with activities that can be done by phone or over the Internet. Use your mindful gauge as well as your common sense to help you to optimize the choice of what you do as well as determining how much and when.

You do not need a big project or publicity to make lemonade. You just have to do something that helps someone else, even just a little. The trick will be to focus on what you can and want to do. Put your sights on your abilities rather than your deficits. For example, my friend Linda, discussed above, could not take on any task that demanded physical ability, but as a skilled listener and social worker she could still help the veterans in her care. Max (Key 5B) became an activist, beginning with just an hour or two a month and gradually increasing his commitment.

Another relevant reason to make lemonade is to provide yourself with activities and projects that will occupy you with something to think about besides trauma. The more productive and involved you become—with family, work, religious group, volunteerism, and so on—the better off you will be. Too many trauma survivors allow its aftermath to engulf whole days of their lives. This is one of the most debilitating things people do in the wake of trauma. It can be downright crippling. I hope that this chapter will inspire and energize you to do something for yourself by helping someone else, countering the effects of trauma through being active and useful.

For making lemonade from lemons, you may find it helpful to draw on several of the previous keys:

- Use mindfulness to zero in on what you might like to do (Key 1).
- Remember that you are able to get involved because you survived (Key 2).
- Make sure to size the steps so you can accomplish them. For instance, if you are not ready to go out to do something, then find things you can do at home, such as supporting someone by phone, home office work, or baking (Key 6).
- Help someone with errands, gardening or the like (Key 7).

The Case

Slight of build and slightly bowed, gray-haired Francine was nearing retirement when the bank she worked in was robbed. She had been an eyewitness to the organized invasion and the shooting of two of her coworkers. The robbers had not harmed her, declaring, "We don't hurt grandmothers!" Nonetheless, she had been so devastated by the incident that she was never able to return to work again.

Francine was at a loss for how to cope with what had happened. Though she had not feared for her own life, the violence and brutality she witnessed were overwhelming for her. She spent more and more time at home and lost interest in previous pleasures, including a local dance club. She just could not face the cheerfulness of the members and the liveliness of the meetings. Her friends became increasingly concerned as she continued to decline their invitations. Since no one she knew had been through anything similar, she felt they could no longer relate to her.

The degree of isolation Francine felt following the robbery is frequent among victims of trauma. Being the only one, or one of few, to experience something so extreme can leave the survivor feeling totally alone. It is one of the reasons that making lemonade by helping others who have suffered something similar can be so helpful to both.

Apply a Little Theory

We have few areas of research in the trauma field that decisively show interventions that help victims of trauma to recover. One area where research results appear fairly clear includes recent studies that identify a sense of purpose as having a huge effect on trauma recovery. That combined with a sense of control appears to have an even greater positive effect. So blending the two, finding purpose and gaining control, through consciously making lemonade makes for a powerful combination.

In the wake of the terrorist attacks of September 11, KNBC TV in Los Angeles set up a call-in trauma hotline staffed by area volunteer psychotherapists. The response was huge. Many, many therapists (including myself) were eager to help. The station was so inundated with volunteers that they had to restrict us each to only a single 4-hour shift. That was frustrating for many who had hoped to have a way to help over several days. I suspect that consciously or unconsciously, most of us knew from previous situations and experience with clients that the more helpfully involved we could become, the better we would cope ourselves. And that proved true for those who were calling in for help also. The ones who were isolated at home (either by choice or physical circumstance) seemed to fare the worst. Those who were able to get out, help others, invite family and friends to their homes, and so on managed much better. I encouraged almost everyone I talked to during my volunteer shift to either go out somewhere where others might be gathering (e.g., church, a restaurant, or community center) or ask someone to come to them (e.g., for coffee, dinner, or to watch a movie).

On that day I was reminded of the reciprocal nature of helping others; it is really a two-way street. The helper gains from the act of helping as much or more than the helpee. For that reason I have never believed in altruism, though that in no way diminishes my enthusiasm for it. The benefit to the giver is just a bonus; it does not lessen the gift. Helping someone else to manage or to feel better will almost always help you.

Discovering the Key

I grew increasingly concerned for Francine's isolation. She could not motivate herself to get together with friends or attend the dancing group. Walks around her neighborhood were her only activity. Sometimes she would briefly, if superficially, chat with adults or children she met on the street. However, the conversations would not last long before she would hurry home, where she felt the most comfortable.

The fact that Francine would periodically complain about the youths who hung about "looking bored" or "on the edge of mischief" gave me hope for her. Despite her anger (or maybe because of it), when she talked about these kids she became much more animated than at any other time during our contacts. I waited a while before pointing this out, hoping my timing would be lucky. When I did finally ask her about it, she agreed. Thinking about how the schools were "falling short" made her feel very "stirred up." I asked if the strength of her feelings had any other origins. She considered that for a moment and then made a connection to her own situation: She wondered if the bank robbers had once been like the local teens, hanging about on her street.

"What if they were?" I asked. "How would you go about changing their destiny?"

Francine was clearly surprised by my question. Of course she had complained to friends and family about the kids' bored sulking. But she had not thought much about what might underlie their apathy or if she could do anything about it.

"I suppose I would try to get them more interested in school, see if they could make a better future for themselves," Francine proposed. We agreed that education was a possible antidote to crime that is generated from boredom and lack of purpose. But we also shared the opinion that it was a condition that she was not likely to be able to change. On the other hand, I suggested, she might be able to make a small dent in it. "Maybe," she said.

An idea was beginning to take shape in my mind. "What was your best subject in school?" I wondered. She was good at mathematics, which was why she had been successful working at the bank, working with numbers. My next question was about the kids. Were there any of them who might be able to use a little help with their math homework? Francine suspected all of them did, but zeroed in on a 12-year-old girl who also seemed somewhat neglected.

"Sometimes I wish I could get my hands on her," Francine confided. "I would love to be able to help her."

"Really? Well, why don't you?" I challenged her. I was actually holding my breath, excited that she was taking to this idea. It had seemed to evolve naturally enough but I did not want to push her into it. However, she appeared to be enthusiastic, something I had never seen in her before.

Our dialogue turned to strategizing how she might approach the girl with an offer of free tutoring. For both their sakes, I suggested they start with a trial meeting of only 15–30 minutes. They could test each other and see if there would be a basis to continue. We discussed and then rehearsed how Francine might approach both the girl to assess her interest and the girl's mother to obtain permission.

The next week Francine looked more lively than I had ever seen her. The girl had been shy, but interested. As the mother did not really care one way or the other, the way was clear. They had a first tutorial and made a date for a second. Through the following weeks, Francine's emotional state improved. She began going to church again, taking the girl with her. They were a good fit, so their relationship grew. The girl provided Francine with companionship and purpose. In return she gradually became a kind of safe harbor for the girl as well as helping her to improve her grades. Over time, Francine became more and more involved in the girl's education and future.

Francine's was not an unusual situation. I have heard similar stories from many: Adults, often retirees, forming bonds with one or more area kids in need of someone to take interest in them. Sometimes they do this through organized programs such as the Big Brother and Big Sister or Foster Grandparents groups. However, many form relationships informally. Several people in my own personal network have done exactly that. One now has an "adopted grandson." Another keeps a close connection with a couple of inner-city teens. Actually, I also had an "adopted mother." Her name was Margie and I dedicated my first book to her. So I know firsthand how valuable it can be for both parties in such relationships.

Applications for You

When you are ready, it would be a good idea to brainstorm something you could do—just a little—for someone else. It might even be a good idea to brainstorm before you feel ready to actually do something, just so you have options prepared ahead of time. There are several ways to approach this, likely more than I will outline in the following exercises. I will start you off with a few ideas in the hope that if none suit you, the examples will inspire you to realize or create what does suit you. Often people suffering from trauma wait and wait for something to change. The longer they wait, the more paralyzed they become. One of the best things you can do for yourself is to do something—almost anything—for someone else. Doing for others will do good for you.

How Will I Know if I Am Ready to Make Lemonade?

It is a little tricky to answer this question. Like nearly everything else we have discussed in this book, the answer is very individual to your circumstances, needs, and body. Your mindful gauge should be a good help here. Imagine scenarios and pay attention to the response of your gauge for guidance. Be forewarned—sometimes getting started with making lemonade is similar to getting started with moving and exercise (see Key 7). At times it can be necessary to push yourself to take the first small step as a way to prime the rest of your steps. That is what I did with Francine, above, in challenging her about the neighbor girl. She was fairly ready to do something, but needed a small prod to get herself in motion. It is not always easy to determine when reluctance means, "No! Not now!" and when it means, "I'd like to take the first step, but can't quite do it." This is where your gauge might prove especially useful, in distinguishing nuances.

In general, consider such things as:

- Do I have enough energy for what I want to do?
- Will I be able to keep my focus?
- How will I handle any eventual anxiety or distress?
- Have I taken care to ensure I will be able to manage the amount of time?

- Am I confident in the task? If not, what do I need to become so?
- Have I arranged for support—a friend or professional to talk with about my experience of helping?
- Is my first step small enough to ensure success?

Exercise 1: Could Someone in Your Neighborhood Use Help?

How about a lonely elderly person who could use a visit now and then or even just help taking out the trash? Is there a child you could tutor, like Francine? Or, for that matter, the dog of an invalid who would love to go for a walk? It does not matter who or what. The goal is to help and, in so doing, to add to your own sense of usefulness and purpose.

Try just one small act of helpfulness and evaluate how you feel. Use your gauge to determine if it is beneficial for you. If you realize a positive effect, then carry on. If you have a negative reaction, look at the task and the timing and consider what would better suit you. Be patient. It may take several experiments before you settle on something that works for both you as helper and the one you are helping.

Do not be discouraged if someone does not want or need your help. There are those who are either shy to accept help or interpret it as weakness. That has nothing to do with you. So take any rejection in stride and offer your help to someone else.

Exercise 2: What Kind of Volunteer Work Could You Do?

Make a list of any kind of volunteer work you might be able to do now or at stages in the future, whether it is only once or on a regular basis, for 10 minutes, half an hour, or half a day. You might need to do a bit of research. The Internet is one way to find groups in need of help. Your local United Way office can be a good place to start. They will know of many organizations. Remember that volunteer work can be done at home or away from it. If you are lacking companionship or fairly isolated, consider an activity that would bring you into contact with others, even if only by telephone. Use your mindful gauge to evaluate what (and when) is best for you.

Exercise 3: What Have You Learned From Your Trauma?

List anything and everything you have learned from your experience that could be useful to someone else. If you have several traumas, you might make separate lists. Focus on the *enabling* aspects rather than the disabling, for example, "I learned to be independent" instead of "I was neglected." For this key to be useful, the emphasis must be on learning that has or could help you or others. How could you use that knowledge to better yourself, someone else, or your world? For example, many of those who were abused as children become highly determined not to hurt their own children and to intervene when they see (or hear of) someone else abusing a child.

Exercise 4: What Can You Take From Your Own Traumatic Experiences That Could Help Another?

Examples of ways your experiences could benefit others might include:

- Cautioning a child or friend on ways they might reduce the likelihood of something you went through, such as rape or assault

- Talking to a friend who is going through something similar to your experience, such as chemotherapy or loss
- Becoming involved in a volunteer organization that helps others who have trauma such as yours, for example, the Red Cross or a rape crisis center

Evaluate This Key

After you have had one or more experiences of helping another—no matter how brief—take time to evaluate if the timing or task has or has not been good for you. Use your mindful gauge to help you determine if you should carry on or if you would be better off changing something or even postponing future attempts.

Plan How to (or Not to) Use This Key

When you find which lemonade-making activities suit you, work out a structure for doing them on a regular basis. What timing works best for you: daily, alternate days, weekly, biweekly, monthly, yearly? Set a date to evaluate how you are faring. Take a look at whether you want to change one or more things you are doing or change the schedule, and so on.

If you decide that it is not a good time for you to make lemonade, set a date when you will revisit the idea for reevaluation. Just because it is not good for you now in no way means that it will not be useful ever. As with most things, good timing is crucial.

Afterword:

Evaluating Recovery Progress

Perhaps you have noticed by now that 8 *Keys To Safe Trauma Recovery* has the potential to ease some of the pressure of your traumatic stress. I hope you have found that many of the keys do just that for you. In general, a traumatized person is similar to a pressure cooker—the higher the pressure, the more difficult it is to manage the system safely. For any method, exercise, or intervention to be successful in facilitating your safe recovery, it must help you to reduce the pressure of your trauma. Just as it is unsafe to open a pressure cooker while the pressure inside is high, it is also unsafe for you to attempt to open up your trauma while filled with pressurized traumatic stress. It is for this reason that on these pages I have emphasized strategies that promote reducing stress and maximizing stabilization.

Measuring Recovery

It is my suggestion that right now you evaluate how your life is going on a day-to-day basis. That will give you a baseline for comparision. Of course all of us have days that go better or worse than others, but there will be general trends. A good tool for such evaluation is the SUDS—Subjective Units of Distress Scale. For example, right now as you read this, how awake are you? Use a scale of 1–10, 10 = wide awake, 1 = being asleep. Right now as I write this sentence, my score is 10. If I were lying in bed reading rather than writing, my score might be close to a 2 or 3. It is as simple as that. You can apply the SUDS to evaluating your state of recovery:

- How calm are you? 1 = the most calm possible, 10 = the worst anxiety possible. What was your score when you began your recovery? What is it now?
- Is there any difference in your ability to focus—on a task, conversation, book, or television program? 1 = best focus, 10 = worst focus. What was your score at the beginning? And now?
- If you have mood swings, have the extremes lessened? 1 = totally normal, 10 = totally extreme. Then? Now?
- Have you had flashbacks? If so, in a similar way, rate both their frequency and severity at the start of recovery and now.
- And so on. You may have indicators for measuring I have not thought of. You can do the same with them.

There will also be objective measures that you can identify with your common sense: Are you sleeping more hours? Are you able to go to work now? And so on.

How the Traumatized Nervous System Heals

There is another important factor to figure into your evaluation: When you get knocked off kilter or upset, how long does it take you to get back to normal now? How about shortly after your trauma or when you began your recovery? Is there a difference? The traumatized nervous system is very slow to normalize. You may have noticed early in your recovery that small disturbances could affect you for days or weeks. As your nervous system heals, those intervals from disturbance to balance will usually get shorter. I cannot promise that you will stop being disturbed by things in your life; everyone's life has upsets and distress at times.

What determines emotional health—and trauma recovery—is how you are able to handle those stresses and how quickly you bounce back from them.

I have heard many clients complain following something disturbing that happened since our last meeting. There is a tendency to describe and be upset about their reaction being just the same as it used to be months (or even years) ago. Often they fear they are regressing to the same point at which they began. However, when I ask how long it took them to get over whatever it was, they nearly always report a relatively shorter time interval. When I remind them how long it used to take to recuperate from such an upset, they are often amazed to realize that they really have improved—often a lot.

So take into account more than that you get upset. Also consider how you handle upset and how quickly you get back your balance. Do not expect to be 100% free of trauma reminders; it is a part of your history. What you should aim for is to no longer be knocked off balance by those reminders.

Next Steps

What will be your next steps? If you find your quality of life and stability improved by the help you have received here or elsewhere, you may decide to put trauma behind you and focus on your future. Some of you may want to use the foundation of your stability to delve into trauma memories. There could also be a portion of you who have not yet found the help you need. I hope you will use your mindful gauge and common sense to aid you in your continued healing pursuits.

I sincerely hope that this book has been of help to you.

Further Reading

This list is purposely brief as I do not want to overload readers who already have overwhelmed nervous systems with too much information. For those of you who would like a more comprehensive library of books on trauma and PTSD, please check first with Glenn Schiraldi's *PTSD Sourcebook*.

Popular

Damasio, Antonio. *Descartes' Error: Emotion, Reason, and the Human Brain*. New York: Avon Books, 1994.

de Becker, Gavin. *The Gift of Fear: And Other Survival Signals That Protect Us From Violence*. New York: Dell, 1997.

Herman, Judith. *Trauma and Recovery: The Aftermath of Violence—From Domestic Abuse to Political Terror*. New York: Basic Books, 1997.

Lamott, Anne. *Bird by Bird: Some Instructions on Writing and Life*. New York: Anchor Books, 1995.

Levine, Peter. *Waking the Tiger: Healing Trauma*. Berkeley, CA: North Atlantic Books, 1997.

Maurer, Robert. *One Small Step Can Change Your Life: The Kaizen Way*. New York: Workman, 1994.

Napier, Nancy. *Getting Through the Day: Strategies for Adults Hurt as Children*. New York: W.W. Norton, 1993.

Sapolsky, Robert M. *Why Zebras Don't Get Ulcers: A Guide to*

Stress, Stress-Related Diseases, and Coping. New York: W.H. Freeman, 1994.

Schiraldi, Glenn. *The PTSD Sourcebook.* 2nd ed. New York: McGraw Hill, 2009.

Professional

Nathanson, Donald. *Shame and Pride: Affect, Sex, and the Birth of the Self.* New York: W.W. Norton, 1992.

Rothschild, Babette. *The Body Remembers: The Psychophysiology of Trauma and Trauma Treatment.* New York: W.W. Norton, 2000.

Rothschild, Babette. *The Body Remembers Casebook: Unifying Methods and Models in the Treatment of Trauma and PTSD.* New York: W.W. Norton, 2003.

Siegel, Daniel. *The Mindful Brain: Reflection and Attunement in the Cultivation of Well-Being.* New York: W.W. Norton, 2007.

van der Kolk, Bessel, ed. *Traumatic Stress: The Effects of Overwhelming Experience on Mind, Body, and Society.* New York: Guilford, 1996.

Notes to Self-Help Readers

You have probably chosen to read this book because you or someone close to you has suffered one or more traumatic events. It is my sincere hope that you will find the information and exercises on these pages to be helpful to you and yours.

Although my case illustrations are composites of people I have encountered in a professional role, all of the keys can be applied outside the realm of psychotherapy. For those of you pursuing trauma recovery via self-help, these keys will help you to design your own safe program. Everything in this book is meant to fit as an adjunct to other philosophies, so you can use this information (or bits of it) alongside other books or programs. You may find these keys to be adequate for what you need, or you may combine them with exercises, theory, or techniques from other sources.

Self-help can be a great way to pursue trauma recovery. The majority of people recover from trauma without therapy or other kinds of professional intervention and have done so since the beginning of time. If you do not have the desire or the money to hire a professional, self-help may be a good choice.

However, one thing a self-help book cannot provide you with is human contact, which has proven to be useful for healing trauma. So you may need to exert some effort to get the support you need to aid your recovery. Use the first key, the mindful gauge, to help you to decide if talking with someone about your recovery journey would be helpful to you. And then use the gauge to help you decide whom to share your experiences with, such as a friend, family member, clergy, or teacher. Having someone to use as a sounding board may help you to organize your thoughts and feelings. It is important to remember that contact and support are highly beneficial to trauma recovery. Just because you are pursuing self-help does not mean you have to do it alone.

That said, also take care with *what* you tell the person or people you decide to talk with. Those who are not professionally trained to help with trauma are usually ill equipped to hear details of horrendous experiences—and it may not be good for you to discuss them either (see Keys 3 and 4). Think in terms of talking with your support person about the difficulties in your life *now* that may or may not stem from your traumatic experiences. And when you do talk with someone about what happened to you, steer away from details, sticking with an overview or headline of what happened instead. Most people will be able to manage hearing that another has, for instance, been emotionally or physically injured. However, hearing the graphic particulars of those injuries or exactly how they occurred step by step could be unnecessarily upsetting for some if not many.

It can also be a good idea to forewarn potential listeners and find out when they have time to listen to you. Most of us know the experience of being upset, calling a friend, and blurting out our feelings only to find out we caught the friend at an inopportune time. The result can be devastating when we are distressed and vulnerable. A better tactic is to ask, "Is this a good time?" When it is not, you can agree on a later one. Inquiring first could spare you adding feelings of rejection and abandonment to your already overloaded plate.

Notes to Past, Present, and Future Clients of Trauma Therapy

Trauma therapy can be a tough process. It is demanding of psychological and physical energy as well as time and money. You can improve your chances of getting value for your investment by:

- Being informed.
- Identifying your needs.
- Recognizing what does and does not help you.

It is for these reasons that I intend *8 Keys to Safe Trauma Recovery* to also serve as a relevant adjunct to your treatment. This is a book that you can make use of on your own, but you can also read and apply it together with your therapist. I have always believed that the best trauma therapy (really any therapy) is a genuine partnership, a cooperative effort of both therapist and client. The more you can work together, the better potential for a good outcome. Therefore I would suggest that this book be one among several adjuncts you make use of together with your therapist. Perhaps you will try one or more exercises alone, though you may find that attempting some of them with the assistance of your therapist is of benefit. At the least, I hope you will discuss with your therapist what you are reading and doing on your own. It is important to specify what you have found that furthers your recovery and what you have identified that hinders it. In addition, the first chapter, "Plot Your Course With Mindfulness," will be helpful in evaluating which therapist you hire as well as appraising the success of the therapy along the way.

I highly recommend that you choose a therapist based on your connection rather than on a particular method or model. Time and again it has been shown that the most important factor in successful therapy is the relationship between client and therapist. That said, a therapist trained in several methods would be preferable over one who has only learned—and therefore is exclusively loyal to—one type of trauma therapy. No one procedure works for all, nor does any single theory apply to everyone. The therapist with only one model to fall back on has nothing else to offer if that does not work. Unfortunately, in such a situation, it is often the client who is blamed for any failure. The best therapist will have broad choices of theory and interventions to use and be able to recommend which to apply to your unique situation, tailoring the therapy to your needs.

Many insurance organizations as well as practitioners support an adherence to a solitary technique by citing its evidence base. Be skeptical. Though research is useful in identifying trends, it is by no means the last word on what is best *for you*. Just because a system has been documented as successful does not guarantee it will work for you. Just about every method of trauma therapy has something to offer. What works for one may not work for another and vice versa. Penicillin provides the best analogy for my argument. Though a miracle drug for many, it is lethal for others. Just as no one antibiotic is a cure-all, so there is not one trauma therapy that will help each and every survivor of trauma. Remember Martha (see Key 1) and use your mindful gauge and common sense to choose what appeals to you. Then evaluate and reevaluate your therapy along the way.

Last, do not let a therapist—or anyone else for that matter—push you to face memories or use techniques against your will, your common sense, or your mindful gauge. Remember that you are the best expert on you. You are the only one with you

24/7. You may need some help to guide you to accurate self-knowledge, but you are the one who ultimately knows what is good for you and what is not. At the same time, remember that you cannot expect a therapist to follow you down a path he or she believes could be dangerous. So even if you think something is absolutely what you need to or should do, you could encounter a therapist who would not agree to do it with you.

Notes to Trauma
Treatment Professionals

8 Keys to Safe Trauma Recovery was written to the survivor of trauma—self-help reader and therapy client alike. The voice of the book is speaking directly to them. However, I hope that you will also find the philosophy and tools in this book of use as an adjunct to your knowledge and methods.

I gained my master's degree in clinical social work in 1976 and pursued a general psychotherapy and body psychotherapy practice for several years before I began specializing in treating traumatized individuals in 1989. I started offering training and consultation to colleagues such as you in 1992. Over the years I have identified several areas for caution that I would like to pass on to you.

First, do not be overly influenced by the *evidence base*. It is meant as a guide, not as law. One of the biggest problems I see in the field of trauma therapy is the tendency to quote the evidence as the last word on what helps or hurts clients. If only it was that simple. Science is just not that exact—witness the medicines and medical treatments that are introduced and withdrawn on a regular basis. And, unfortunately, outcome studies—for better or for worse—are among the most biased research there is. However, arguing this point is irrelevant. Even if scientific evaluation was perfectly controlled, still there would never be any single method that would heal every trauma survivor, just as there is no single antidepressant that helps everyone, or even a majority. Thank goodness we have a wide variety of theories and methods to study and apply. Considering multiple tools is the only way to discover what helps an individual. Maybe it means taking a little from this and a lot from that. I wish that heaps of common sense would always be an ingredient.

Beware common mistakes of trauma therapy:

- *Give ample time to Phase I (stabilizing) work.* Sometimes when I teach or lecture on this topic, therapists will ask when I will get to the "real" trauma work. That always amazes me, as I regard the work we do to stabilize and make our clients safe as the *most important* real trauma work we can do. Often problems that arise are simply solved by revisiting this stage of trauma treatment or giving it more time.

- *Contain curiosity.* One of the most important tools you can have as a trauma professional is the ability to contain your curiosity. If you cannot restrain your need to know you could prematurely (if unconsciously) push your clients into discussing material they are not ready to face. Providing details of horrible events will be contraindicated for many of them. The only reason to ask for details is when processing such details will further a client's recovery.

- *Learn to pare down step size.* Much of the frustration of trauma therapy is the result of steps being more than the client can manage. Frequently, what is actually too much for the client is misinterpreted as resistance. It does not matter whether it is the therapist or client designing the step. If success is evasive, reducing the pace could make a big difference.

- *Bypassing current trauma to focus on past trauma.* If your client improved with Phase I work but is now getting worse, reevaluate what you are working on. Is it what the client came in with, the current situation that motivated him to seek help? Or did you get distracted by an earlier trauma history? This is not an uncommon scenario and is responsible for many instances of client decline. One of the best tenets from the early years of psychotherapy is to always ask the client, "Why now? What was it that tipped the balance in your decision to get therapy?" That reason is always important. Even if there is a clear history of trauma, the recent event or situation that brought the client in needs attention. If you backtrack there, you may recoup your client's earlier improvement as well as trust. After the referring issue is resolved, approaching an earlier trauma will be much safer.

- *Do not assume that what was helpful for you will be helpful for your clients.* This is one of the biggest mistakes we make as professionals. Of course what has helped us may be helpful to some of our clients. But jumping to the conclusion that what is good for you is good for them could cause you both lots of frustration. I often smile when I hear a colleague moan, "I know just what would help, but my client is resistant." The more accurate statement would usually be, "I know just what would help me in that situation." That is quite a difference. Projection is great for giving us ideas, but never mistake it for truth.

- *Do not allow clients to push you to address memories with them prematurely, or to take any other steps you do not believe they (or you) are ready for.* Most of us have regrets—I certainly do—for times we have let our best judgment be deterred. Listen to your own wisdom and common sense to reduce the chance of doing damage to your client (and yourself). Remember the medical precept: First do no harm.

- *Maintain continuity of care.* You may think it unnecessary for me to write this, but I have heard of far too many situations where this basic principle was not followed, and thus feel that I must mention it. The number of clients I have heard of being left high and dry by their therapists is of great concern. Many clients, especially traumatized clients, have reduced capacity and resources for getting the help they need. For many of them, that is why they are still suffering from trauma in the first place. All of us encounter clients we cannot help. If you become frustrated in working with one or more clients to the point that you no longer believe you can help them, make sure to secure referrals before you terminate with them.

Last, do not forget to take care of yourself. Trauma therapy is very taxing on the emotional and physical reserves of the therapist. Many of the keys in this book may also help you. For instance, pay attention to your own mindful gauges to help you identify when you need to slow down, take a break, take a vacation, and so on. Exercise as well as increased muscle tone may also help you to better manage the stress of your work. For more on this, you may find my book *Help for the Helper* to be of interest.

Index

activity(ies), physical. *see* physical
    activity
adequate level of functioning, on
    daily basis, in trauma recov-
    ery, 54
adversity(ies), dealing with,
    131–43
  activities and projects in,
    133–35
  applications, 139–40
  case example, 131–33, 135–39
  discovering key, 137–39
  doing for others in, 132–34,
    136–37
  evaluation of key, 143
  exercises for, 141–43
  guidelines for, 134–35, 140–
    41
  helping others, exercise for,
    141
  how to use key, 143
  lessons learned from, applica-
    tions to others, 142–43
  organizations in, 133–34
  sense of purpose in, 136–37
  terrorism of September 11,
    2001, 136
  timing in, 132, 134

Aesop, 111
Aesop's Fables, 107
agoraphobia, 121
Alexander technique, mindfulness
    in, 12
Allen, W., 12
Amber Alert Program, 134
American Cancer Society, 134
America's Most Wanted, 134
amygdala
  decision making by, information
    related to, 79
  function of, 30–31, 79–80
  orders of, stress hormones in
    delivering, 79–80
  response to stress, 93
  in survival, 79
Annie Hall, 11–12
anxiety
  high level, case example,
    108–11
  relaxation effects on, 122–23
Aristotle, 7
attempted robbery, response to,
    case example, 118–19
avoidance
  measured, value of, 105–7
  metered, value of, 105–7

avoiding eye contact, as response
        to shame, 88–89
awareness
    body, in decision making, 13–
        14
    emotional, in decision making,
        13–14

balance, described, 64
bank robbery, trauma due to, deal-
        ing with, case example,
        135–39
Beatles, "Come Together," 14
Big Brother program, 139
Big Sister program, 139
bigger leaps, smaller steps for,
        101–14. *see also* smaller
        steps
*Bird by Bird: Some Instructions on
        Writing and Life,* 101
body, mindfulness in, 12–13
body awareness, in decision mak-
        ing, 13–14
body psychotherapies, mindfulness
        in, 12
body reactions, to touch, mindful-
        ness in, 15–18
bombing, terrorist, trauma recov-
        ery after, case example,
        45–47
brain, emotional response system
        of, amygdala in, 31
breathing, in discovering mindful
        gauge, 20
Buddha, mindfulness taught by,
        foundations of, 12–13
burglary, response to, case exam-
        ple, 118–19
business acumen, sharpening of,
        in depression management,
        12

case examples
    Beth, taking smaller steps,
        107–8
    Eileen, dealing with shame, 89,
        91, 94, 99
    Francine, finding purpose and
        gaining control, 135–41
    Gary, taking smaller steps,
        108–11
    Helen, forgiving yourself, 77–78
    Jack, importance of physical
        exercise, 116–17, 119–20
    Janice, managing touch, 11–12,
        15–20
        as example of multiple trau-
            ma, unstable survivor, 54,
        as example of setting goals
            beyond reach, 103
    Josh, feeling guilty for not fight-
        ing back, 80–84, 93–95
    Kate, physical exercise to
        overcome chronic freeze,
        118–20
    Liam, stopping flashbacks,
        62–64, 67–69
    Lilly, taking smaller steps,
        104–5
    Martha, using mindfulness, and
        common sense, 10–11, 154
    Max, sharing shame to manage
        PTSD, 90–91, 93, 95–96,
        134
    Meco, taking smaller steps,
        104–5
    Peter, forgiving your limitations,
        75
    Rosa, managing steps by put-
        ting one or more aside, or
        changing them, 105–7,
        113
    Sandra, forgiving yourself, 74

Stuart, recovering without remembering, 45–48, 53
Tina, increasing muscle tone
to feel more protection,
123–24
chart(s), for graphing exercise,
124–25
cognitive therapies, mindfulness
in, 12
"Come Together," 14
common sense
defined, ix
mindfulness and, 25–26
in trauma recovery, ix–xi
communication
about forgiveness and self-
forgiveness, exercise for,
85
about shame, guidelines for,
96–98
concentration difficulties
PTSD and, 28
trauma and, 28
confidence, in mindfulness decisions, 16–17
consciousness, focus of, in mindfulness, 13
containment, increase in, exercise
for, 119–20
control, lack of, trauma and,
76–77
coping mechanisms, weakening
of, focus on past trauma
and, 51–52
Couric, K., 73
court system, in freeze response,
84
crime(s), hate, self-forgiveness
related to, case example,
80–81
cutting, case example, 105–7

Damasio, A., 13–15
Damasio's theory of somatic markers, 13–14
decision making
body awareness in, 13–14
emotional awareness in, 13–14
mindfulness in, confidence,
16–17
Department of Veterans Affairs
(VA), 95
depression
exercise effects for, 115–16
management of, mindfulness
in, 12
Descartes' Error, 13
destabilization, focusing on, past
trauma and, 51–52
dharmas, mindfulness in, 12
dialogue, inner, in trauma recovery, 59–60
dissociation, mindfulness in,
17–18
doing for others, in dealing with
adversity, 132–34, 136–
37
ducking head, as response to
shame, 88–89

eating disorders
PTSD and, 28
trauma and, 28
elevator(s), fear of, case example,
109–11
emotional awareness, in decision
making, 13–14
emotional exhaustion, case example, 108–11
emotional instability, increase in,
in trauma healing, 43
emotional response system, of
brain, amygdala in, 31

epilogue, beginning with, in trauma recovery, 27–41
    applications, 34–35
    case example, 29–35
    celebrating survival in, 38
    in confirming actual outcomes, 34
    discovering key in, 32–34
    evaluating key, 38–39
    exceptions for, 36
    exercises for, 36–38
    hippocampal role in, 30–34
    how to use key, 39
    mantra in, 36–37
    writing of, 35, 37
evidence base, described, 157
evolution, shame in, 87
exercise. *see also* get moving
    as antidote to persistent freeze response, 117–19, 122
    applications, 126
    benefits of, 117–24
        case example, 116–19
        chart for graphing, 124–25
        for physical health, 115–16
    criteria for, 126–27
    in depression management, 115–16
    to dissipate buildup of stress hormones, 120
    evaluation of key, 128
    find buddy for, 128
    find your activity, 127
    to help regulation ongoing stress levels, 120
    how to use key, 128–29
    to increase containment and self-control via increased muscle tone, 119–20
    for PTSD
        benefits of, 116

    case example, 121
    record keeping in, 127–28
    for trauma victims, benefits of, 116
exercise buddy, 128
exhaustion, emotional, case example, 108–11
external reality, 64–67
external senses, 64, 67–68
eye contact, avoiding of, as response to shame, 88–89

false memories, creation of, 58
fear(s)
    case example, 108–11
    of elevators, 109–11
    of heights, 109–11
    of shower, case example, 105–7
feelings
    about touch, mindfulness in, 15–18
    in discovering mindful gauge, 20
    mindfulness in, 12–13
Feldenkrais, mindfulness in, 12
fight-or-flight response, case example, 80–82
flashback(s)
    categorization of, 60–61
    defined, 34
    described, 60
    full-blown, case example, 30
    interceding during, steps in, 66
    language in, changing experience with, 61–62
    as memory of event, 60–62
    in PTSD, 60
    sensory system in, 64–67
    stopping of, 59–72
        applications, 68–69

case example, 62–63, 67–68
discovering key, 67–68
evaluation of key, 71–72
exercises for, 69–71
how to use key, 72
mantras in, 69–70
perceiving safety in, 66
protocol for, 70–71
steps in, 66
talking about, as if in present, 60
forgiveness. *see also* self-forgiveness
applications, 82–83
case example, 77–78, 80–81
evaluation of key, 85
exercises for, 83–85
how to use key, 85
put yourself in someone else's shoes, exercise for, 84
shame and reconciling, 73–100. *see also* shame
talk with others about, exercise for, 85
of your limitations, 73–87
Foster Grandparents program, 139
freeze response
case example, 81–83
counteracting, exercise in, 117–19, 122
legitimacy of, recognition by society and law, 84
full-blown flashbacks, case example, 30

gauge(s), mindful. *see* mindful gauge
Gavin, M., ix
Gestalt therapy, mindfulness in, 12

get moving, 115–29. *see also* exercise
applications, 126
benefits of, 117–24
case example, 118–19
chart for graphing, 124–25
criteria for, 126–27
to dissipate buildup of stress hormones, 120
evaluation of key, 128
exercise buddy in, 128
exercise(s) for, 127–28
find your activity, 127
to help regulate ongoing stress levels, 120
how to use key, 128–29
to increase containment and self-control via increased muscle tone, 119–20
record keeping in, 127–28
goal(s)
beyond reach, danger of setting, case example, 103
huge, overwhelming, of traumatized individuals, 107–8
step down, exercise for, 113
in trauma recovery, 43–44
of trauma self-help books and therapies, 44

Hakomi, mindfulness in, 12
Hall, M., 101
hate crime, self-forgiveness related to, case example, 80–81
head, ducking of, as response to shame, 88–89
healing
power of human contact in, 96
trauma. *see* trauma healing
health, physical, exercise for, benefits of, 115–16

hearing, in discovering mindful
    gauge, 20
height(s), fear of, case example,
    109–11
Help for the Helper, 160
helping others
    after terrorism of September 11,
        2001, 132, 136–37
    exercise for, 141
    taking from own traumatic ex-
        periences in, 142–43
Herman, J., 42
hippocampus
    function of, 30–32
    response to stress, 93
    suppressed, during trauma,
        63–64
    in survival, 79
    during trauma, 63
hormone(s), stress
    amygdala's orders via, 79–80
    buildup of, dissipation of, get
        moving in, 120
human contact, power of, in heal-
        ing and easing deep feel-
        ings of shame, 96
Hurricane Katrina, helping others
        following, 132
hyper startle response
    PTSD and, 28
    trauma and, 28
hypervigilance
    PTSD and, 28
    trauma and, 28

image(s), in discovering mindful
        gauge, 20
impatience, with trauma healing,
        102
incest, shame of, 91

Indian Ocean tsunami (December
        2004), 77
individuality, in trauma recovery,
        xi
inner dialogue, in trauma recov-
        ery, 59–60
instability, emotional, increase in,
        in trauma healing, 43
integration, in trauma recovery,
        importance of, 47–48
internal reality, 64–67
internal senses, 64, 67
intrusion(s), defined, 34
intrusive memories
    PTSD and, 28
    trauma and, 28

Janet, P., 42–45
Janet's model, in trauma recovery,
        42–45

KNBC TV, in Los Angeles, 136

Laing, R.D., 7
Lamott, A., 101, 103, 111
language, in changing flashback
        experience, 61–62
law(s), in free response, 84
lemonade, 131–43. *see also* adver-
        sity, dealing with
Levine, P., 28
lifestyle(s), sedentary, described,
        115–16
limbic system, structures of, 30–31
limitation(s), forgiveness of, 73–
        87
Lincoln, A., Pres., 115
Los Angeles Department of Veter-
        ans Affairs, 131–32
Lowitz, L., 131, 132, 134

MADD. *see* Mothers Against
    Drunk Driving (MADD)
make lemonade, 131–43. *see also*
    adversity(ies), dealing with
mantra(s)
    in beginning with your epi-
        logue, 36–37
    in stopping flashbacks, 69–70
Matthew Shepard Foundation,
    134
measured avoidance, value of,
    105–7
memory(ies)
    false, creation of, 58
    flashbacks as, 60–62
    intrusive
        PTSD and, 28
        trauma and, 28
    trauma. *see* trauma memories
memory bypass, memory process-
    ing vs., 43
memory processing, memory by-
    pass vs., 43
metered avoidance, value of,
    105–7
midbrain, structures in, 30–31
mind, mindfulness in, 12–13
mindful gauge
    defined, 14
    discovering, exercise for, 21–22
    identifying, 15–20
    practicing to plot your course,
        24
    practicing with benign choices,
        exercise for, 22–23
    practicing with more relevant
        choices, exercise for, 23–24
mindfulness, 7–26
    applications, 18–21
    body in, 12–13

Buddha's teaching of, founda-
    tions of, 12–13
case example, 8–9, 11–12,
    15–18
common sense and, 25–26
components of, 15
concept of, 7–8
confidence in, 16–17
in depression management,
    12
described, 7–8, 13
dharmas in, 12
in discovering mindful gauge,
    15–20
dissociation and, 17–18
exercises for, 21–24
feelings in, 12–13
focus of consciousness in, 13
foundations of, exercise for,
    21–22
historical background of, 7,
    12
mind in, 12–13
plot course with, 7–26
    evaluation of, 24–25
    how to use key, 25
    mindful gauge in, exercises
        for, 23–24
practice of, techniques and
    treatments using, 12
in PTSD management, 9
in sharpening business acumen,
    12
somatic markers in, relevance
    of, 14–15. *see also* somatic
    markers
in trauma recovery, 7–26. *see
    also* mindfulness, plot
    course with
treatment program vs., 10–11

"Miracle on the Hudson," 73
Mothers Against Drunk Driving
        (MADD), 133–34
moving, get, 115–29. *see also* get
        moving
multiple trauma
    stable, processing memory of,
        decision for, 53
    unstable, processing memory of,
        decision for, 53–54
    case example, 54
muscle tension, described, 119
muscle tone
    in discovering mindful gauge,
        20
    increase in
        exercise for, 119–20
        in PTSD victims, benefits of,
        123–24
My Big Fat Greek Wedding, 41

nervous system, traumatized, heal-
        ing of, 146–47
Nietzsche, 27

objective measures, in successful
        trauma recovery, 3
outcome, confirmation of, identi-
        fying epilogue in, 34

pacing, in trauma healing
    guidelines for, 102–14
    necessity of, 107
pacing recovery, self-forgiveness
        and, 86
panic attacks, case example, 30,
        105–7
past trauma, focusing on
    coping mechanisms weakening
        due to, 51–52
    effects on present life, 50–51

patience with yourself, self-forgive-
        ness and, 86
phase-oriented approach, to trau-
        ma healing, 42
physical activity
    finding your, 127
    in trauma recovery, 115–29. *see
        also* exercise; get moving
    types of, selection of, 127
physical health, exercise for, ben-
        efits of, 115–16
physical withdrawal, as response to
        shame, 88–89
posttraumatic stress disorder
        (PTSD). *see* PTSD (post-
        traumatic stress disorder)
power of human contact, in heal-
        ing and easing deep feel-
        ings of shame, 96
present life, focusing on past ef-
        fects on, 50–51
pressure cooker, traumatized per-
        sons similarity to, 145
professional(s), trauma treatment,
        notes to, 157–60. *see also*
        trauma treatment profes-
        sionals
progressive relaxation, case ex-
        ample, 120
proprioception, described, 64–65
psychological, defined, 10
psychotherapy(ies), body, mindful-
        ness in, 12
PTSD (posttraumatic stress disor-
        der)
    acceptance of, 92–93
    candidates for, 93
    characteristics of, 35
    dealing with, 132–33
    described, 9, 63
    features of, 27

freeze response due to, exercise in counteracting, 117–19, 122

increasing muscle tone in victims of, benefits of, 123–24

management of
case example, 9
exercise in, effects of, 116. *see also* exercise; get moving

prevalence of, 93

shame related to
case example, 90–91
dealing with, case example, 95–96

stress in, 92

symptoms of, 9, 118

trauma flashbacks in, 60

Purple Heart, 96

purpose, sense of, in dealing with adversity, 136–37

put yourself in someone else's shoes, forgiveness-related, exercise for, 84

quality of life, improving, as goal in trauma recovery, 2, 43–44

"R," 75

rape, shame related to, 89

Reach to Recovery, 134

reality
external, 64–67
internal, 64–67

record keeping, of exercise, 127–28

recovery, trauma. *see* trauma recovery

refusal, phrasing of, examples of, 50

Reimert, L., 66

relaxation
anxiety from, 122–23
progressive, case example, 120

remembering, not required, 41–58. *see also* trauma memories

resolved trauma, processing memory of, decision for, 52–53

resources, in trauma recovery, 149–50

responsibility, allocation of, 73–75

robbery
attempted, response to, case example, 118–19
bank, trauma due to, dealing with, case example, 135–39

safety
perceiving of, in stopping flashbacks, 66
in trauma recovery, 48–49

seclusion, as response to shame, 88–89

sedentary lifestyle, described, 115–16

self-control, increase in, exercise for, 119–20

self-forgiveness, 73–87. *see also* forgiveness
applications, 82–83
case example, 74–75, 77–78, 80–81
evaluation of key, 85
hate crime and, case example, 80–81
how to use key, 85
pacing your recovery and, 86
patience with yourself and, 86
put yourself in someone else's shoes, exercise for, 84

self-forgiveness (*continued*)
    talk with others about, exercise
        for, 85
    in trauma recovery, 74
self-help books, trauma-related,
        primary goal of, 44
self-help readers, notes to, 151–52
sensations, in discovering mindful
        gauge, 20
sense(s)
    common. *see* common sense
    external, 64, 67–68
    internal, 64, 67
    in triggering somatic markers,
        14
    types of, 64, 67–68
sense of purpose, in dealing with
        adversity, 136–37
sensory system, in flashbacks,
        64–67
September 11, 2001, terrorism of
    dealing with, 136
    helping others following, 132,
        136–37ad
shame
    absence of, as disadvantage,
        87–88
    addressing of, timing of, 98–99
    apportioning fairly, exercise for,
        99
    aspects of, 88
    dealing with
        power of human contact in,
            96
        steps in, case examples,
            94–96
    dissipation of, 92
    forgiveness and, reconciling of,
        73–100
    hippocampus's response to, 93
    in human evolution, 87

of incest, 91
as indicator of wrong, case ex-
        amples, 89–92
message of, 87
physical responses to, 88–89
PTSD-related, 90–91
    dealing with, case example,
        95–96
rape-related, 89
resolving, 92
in shaping socialization, 91
sharing, 87–100
    exercise for, 100
specifics of, 91–92
as survival function, 89
talking about, guidelines for,
        96–98
trauma-related
    applications, 96–99
    case examples, 89–91
    causes of, 88
    described, 88
    evaluation of key, 100
    exercises for, 99–100
    how to use key, 100
    prevalence of, 88
value of, exercise for, 99
shamelessness, problem of, 87–88
shower(s), fear of, case example,
        105–7
sight, in discovering mindful
        gauge, 20
single trauma, decision for, 53
60 *Minutes*, 73
sleep disturbances
    PTSD and, 28
    trauma and, 28
"slow and steady wins the race,"
        107
small accomplishments, building
        on, 103

smaller steps, 101–14
  applications, 111–12
  case example, 101, 104–5
  contraindication to, 111–12
  evaluation of key, 114
  exercises for, 112–14
  how to use key, 114
  one thing at a time, exercise for,
    112–13
  reducing step to, exercise for,
    112
  step down goal, exercise for,
    113
  temporarily remove or replace
    upsetting task, exercise for,
    113–14
  value of metered or measured
    avoidance in, 105–7
socialization, shame shaping, 91
somatic, defined, 10
somatic markers
  Damasio's theory of, 13–14
  described, 13–14
  mindfulness effects on, 15
  purpose of, 14
  triggering of, 14
somatic treatment methods, mind-
    fulness in, 12
Speed, J., 115
stability
  ensuring of, before dealing with
    trauma memories, 42–43
  essentials necessary for, 48
  evaluation of, exercises for, 56
  increasing, tools for, 56–57
step(s), smaller, 101–14. see also
    smaller steps
Stephanie, 29–37, 53, 66
stress
  amygdala's response to, 93
  defined, 92

in PTSD, 92
  regulation of, exercise in, 120
  traumatic, causes of, 92–93
stress hormones
  amygdala's orders via, 79–80
  buildup of, dissipation of, get
    moving in, 120
stress levels, ongoing, get moving
    in regulation of, 120
stress response, traumatic, 93
subjective measures, in successful
    trauma recovery, 3
Subjective Units of Distress Scale
    (SUDS), in measuring re-
    covery, 145
SUDS (Subjective Units of Dis-
    tress Scale), in measuring
    recovery, 145
Sullenberger, C. "Sully," 73–74
survival
  amygdala in, 79
  celebrating, exercise for, 38
  defined, 79
  hippocampus in, 79
  recognizing, 35
  shame and, 89
survivor(s), trauma, shame in,
    87–100. see also shame
swim, learning to, steps in, case
    example, 104–5

task(s), upsetting, temporarily re-
    move or replace, exercise
    for, 113–14
temperature, in discovering mind-
    ful gauge, 20
tension, muscle, described, 119
terrorism, of September 11, 2001
  dealing with, 136
  helping others following, 132,
    136–37

terrorist bombing, trauma recovery
    after, case example, 45–47
The Body Remembers, 70
thoughts, in discovering mindful
    gauge, 20
three-pronged system, to trauma
    healing, 42
timing, in dealing with adversity,
    132, 134
Tortoise and the Hare, 107
touch, feelings about, mindfulness
    in, 15–18
trauma
    aftermath of, vulnerability in, 10
    characteristics of, 34–35
    exercise effects for, 116
    hippocampus during, 63
    lack of control in, 76–77
    lessons learned from, exercise
        for, 142
    multiple. *see* multiple trauma
    past, focusing on
        coping mechanisms weaken-
            ing due to, 51–52
        effects on present life, 50–51
    physical indicators of, 28
    prevention of, obstacles in, 77
        case example, 77–78
        list of, 77–78
    recounting story of, in PTSD,
        27
    resolved, processing memory of,
        decision for, 52–53
    single, decision for, 53
    symptoms of, 118
Trauma and Recovery, 42
trauma flashbacks. *see* flashback(s)
trauma healing
    emotional instability in, 43
    goal of, xi
    horrendous experience of, ix–x

hurrying of, 102
impatience with, 102
pacing in
    guidelines for, 102–14
    necessity of, 107
phase-oriented approach to, 42
three-pronged system for, 42
trauma memories
    dealing with, methods of, 41–
        58
    ensuring stability prior to deal-
        ing with, 42–43
    focusing on
        applications, 55–56
        destabilization due to, 51–
            52
        discovering key in, 54
        evaluation of key, 58
        exercises for, 56–57
        how to use key, 58
        identifying trauma type in,
            57
        model for deciding to, 52–54
        multiple trauma
            stable, 53
            unstable, 53–54
        pros and cons for, chart in,
            57
        reasons for, 55
        resolved trauma issues, 52–53
        single trauma, 53
    needs and capacities related to,
        identification of, 44–45
    revisiting
        desire for, 49–50
        reasons for not, 50–52
        usefulness of, 41
    strong pull of, 34–35
    trauma recovery without pro-
        cessing, case example,
        45–47

trauma recovery. *see also specific components, e.g.,* self-forgiveness
  common sense in, ix-xi. *see also* common sense
  components of, 2
    keys in, goals of, 2
  epilogue in, beginning with, 27–41. *see also* epilogue, beginning with, in trauma recovery
  exercise effects for, 116. *see also* exercise; get moving
  goal in, 43–44
  improving quality of life in, 43–44
  individual experience in, xi
  integration in, importance of, 47–48
  key issues in, x
  maintaining adequate level of functioning on daily basis in, 54
  making lemonade, 131–43. *see also* adversity(ies), dealing with
  measuring of, 145–46
  nervous system healing in, 146–47
  next steps in, 147
  notes to clients in, 153–55
  physical activity in, 115–29. *see also* exercise; get moving
  progress in
    evaluation of, 145–47
    measuring of, 145–46
    SUDS in, 145–46
  remembering not required in, 41–58. *see also* trauma memories
  resources for, 149–50
  safety in, 48–49
  self-forgiveness in, 73–87
  sense of purpose in, 136–37
  stability in, essentials in, 48–49
  starting point in, 27–41. *see also* epilogue, beginning with, in trauma recovery
  successful
    defined, 3
    objective measures in, 3
    subjective measures in, 3
  task of, overwhelmed by, 102
  without processing memories of event, case example, 45–47
trauma response, neurobiology of, 78–79
trauma self-help books, primary goal of, 44
trauma survivors, shame in, 87–100. *see also* shame
trauma therapies
  clients of, notes to, 153–55
  primary goal of, 44
trauma treatment professionals
  guidelines for, 157–60
  mistakes made by, 158–60
  notes to, 157–60
trauma victims
  huge, overwhelming goals of, 107–8
  similarity to pressure cooker, 145
traumatic stress, causes of, 92–93
traumatic stress response, 93
traumatized nervous system, healing of, 146–47
treatment program, mindfulness vs., 10–11

upsetting task, temporarily remove or replace, exercise for, 113–14

Veterans Affairs (VA), Los Angeles
        Department of, 131–32
victim(s). *see* trauma victims
Vietnam veterans, PTSD in, deal-
        ing with, 95–96
volunteer work, types of, exercise
        for, 141–42
vulnerability, in aftermath of
        trauma, 10

Waking the Tiger, 28
wasp(s), attack by, case example,
        29–35
Welch, C., 115
"when life gives you lemons make
        lemonade," 131–43. *see
        also* adversity, dealing
        with
writing, of epilogue, 35, 37